A YOUR BODY, YOURSELF BOOK

Your Body, Yourself Q&A

by Alison Bell

Illustrated by Wendy Wahman and Mary Bryson

Reviewed and endorsed by Dr. Andrea Wilson and Dr. Tammy Middlebrook, members of the Colorado Medical Society and fellows of the American Academy of Pediatrics

LOWELL

NTC/Co   ...shing Group

To my daughter, Elizabeth
—A.B.

Published by Lowell House
A division of NTC/Contemporary Publishing Group, Inc.
4255 West Touhy Avenue, Lincolnwood (Chicago), Illinois 60646-1975
U.S.A.

Managing Director and Publisher: Jack Artenstein
Director of Publishing Services: Rena Copperman
Editorial Director: Brenda Pope-Ostrow
Director of Juvenile Development: Amy Downing
Cover Photograph: Ann Bogart
Cover Model: Angela Lew
Typesetting & Design: Carolyn Wendt

Lowell House books can be purchased at special discounts
when ordered in bulk for premiums and special sales.
Please contact Customer Service at:
NTC/Contemporary Publishing Group
4255 W. Touhy Avenue
Lincolnwood, IL 60646-1975
1-800-323-4900

Printed and bound in the United States of America

Library of Congress Catalog Card Number: 98-75622

ISBN: 0-7373-0190-2

DHD
10 9 8 7 6 5 4 3 2 1

CONTENTS

Your Body, Yourself Q&A will clear up a lot of questions you have about your feelings and about growing up. However, no book can answer every question you might have as you enter your teen years. If you have a question you need answered, don't be afraid to talk to an adult about it—especially your mom or dad! You may even want to sit down with a parent and read through parts of this book together.

This book is not intended to treat, diagnose, or prescribe. For any physical problems you think you may have, talk to your doctor. If you feel you may have a serious emotional problem, consult a licensed psychological counselor.

Help! I'm (gulp) Growing Up

You've probably always been curious. But now you have a reason to be feeling more curious than ever. Why are you feeling so up and down? Why is your body changing? How come your best friend's got a chest and you're still flat? Does the guy in biology hate you or love you? And above all, **ARE YOU NORMAL?**

Growing up and hitting **puberty** can be very confusing. Sometimes you may feel like you are the first girl on Earth to go through it.

But rest assured, you're not alone. And also know that the changes you're feeling or experiencing are completely normal.

Hopefully, this book will help you realize this. It contains some of the most frequently asked questions preteens and young teens want to know. You can read about your period, body changes, sex, and boys, as well as get the scoop on nutrition, eating disorders, exercise, beauty, drugs, and alcohol. Key words about your body that are explained in the glossary at the back of the book are set in **boldface** type throughout the text.

This book should help you deal with most any issue that comes your way during puberty. I also hope that the pages will inspire and encourage you. Despite some of your overwhelming feelings, this is a very exciting time. You've got a lot to enjoy and look forward to, beginning *right now*.

Get ready for some of the BEST years of your life!

Alison Bell

CHAPTER 1

What's Going On?

When I was in seventh grade, my gym teacher, Mrs. Howells, gave our PE class a lecture on sex education. When she asked how many of us knew the definition of the word puberty, a lot of the girls raised their hands. So I did, too, because I didn't want to be left out.

But inside, I was shaking. Sure, I had a very general idea of what puberty was, but beyond that, I was clueless. The whole time Mrs. Howells talked, I looked down at my feet to make sure she didn't call on me to help explain any of the technicalities. I didn't want to be exposed as a fraud.

After class, one of the girls who had raised her hand asked me, "Did you really know all about that puberty stuff?"

I hesitated a moment, then confessed the truth. "No," I replied.

"Really?" she smiled. "Me neither."

Q. What is puberty? I think I know, but I'm not 100 percent sure.

A. Puberty is a series of changes your body goes through as it matures physically and sexually. While you may not plan on having children for 10 or 20 years, your body is getting ready to produce babies.

Most girls enter puberty between the ages of 9 and 14. Some even start as young as 8. During puberty, you grow taller and your body fills out, you sprout breasts and body hair, and you begin to menstruate, which is the monthly passage of blood and tissue through the **vagina**.

F ASCINATING ACTOID

Girls start puberty sooner than boys. They generally reach puberty between the ages of 9 and 14, boys between 11 and 16.

Q. *How long does puberty last?*

A. Some girls may zip through puberty in one year. Other girls may go through it for five or six years. It all depends on your body. The average time is two years. Here's what you can expect along the way:

❀ As puberty begins, your nipples become enlarged and you start to develop breast buds, which will grow into full breasts. You also grow your first pubic hair and experience a rapid growth in height and weight.

❀ Your breasts grow more fully, and you sprout more pubic hair. You grow underarm hair, and your sweat glands "turn on," causing you to perspire more than you used to. Your skin becomes more oily, and **you may discover your first** pimple.

❀ Your weight and height continue to increase. Your breasts continue to develop, and your nipples may protrude. Your pubic hair grows in almost fully, and you start your period, which is another way of saying you begin **menstruation**.

❀ You are through puberty when your breasts reach their full size and you have established a regular period.

Keep in mind that this timetable varies slightly depending on the girl. Your breasts may develop first; another girl's first sign of puberty may be the appearance of pubic hair. That's because every girl's body is unique.

Q. *What causes puberty to start?*

A. Puberty is triggered by the release of chemical substances in your body called **hormones**. These are responsible for the many changes your body is going through as well as for some of the see-saw emotions you experience during your preteen and teen years. No one knows exactly what "turns on" the puberty hormones. However, the sequence of events happening within every girl's body is the same. Here's how it works:

1 The part of your brain called the **hypothalamus** starts producing a hormone called **gonadotropin-releasing hormone (GnRH)**. This hormone travels to another part of your brain called the **pituitary gland**.

2 The pituitary gland then releases two other hormones, **luteinizing hormone (LH)** and **follicle-stimulating hormone (FSH),** into your bloodstream. These hormones travel to your **ovaries**, the reproductive organs in your body that contain hundreds of thousands of egg cells, the very seeds of life.

3 The LH and FSH cause your ovaries to turn on. The ovaries then produce other hormones, primarily **estrogen** and **progesterone**. Estrogen and progesterone cause many of the physical changes you experience during puberty, including breast development, widening hips, and menstruation.

4 Meanwhile, your left and right **adrenal glands**, each sitting on top of a kidney, produce other hormones

called **androgens**, male sex hormones all men and women produce. These are responsible for other changes during puberty, including growth spurts, acne, and the appearance of underarm and pubic hair.

Q. *I am almost 12 and haven't started going through puberty yet. It seems like all my friends have; a lot of them are even wearing bras! Do you think something is wrong with me?*

A. Not at all! You fall completely into the normal range. Keep in mind that your body is unlike anyone else's. Each girl follows her own timetable. Sure, some girls started puberty before you, while others will start after you. In addition, your

first signs of puberty may be different from those of other girls. Your breasts may develop first; another girl may first sprout pubic hair. However, if you have special concerns, **it's best to see your doctor just to be SAFE.**

Q. *Even though I'm not even 13, I look and feel very adult. I love to hang out with older teens because kids my age seem like babies. My parents tell me I should slow down and not be in such a hurry to grow up. What do you think?*

A. Even though your body may look grown-up, mentally and emotionally, you are still a child and not ready for the responsibilities, pressures, and worries that older teens have to deal with. Besides, are the kids your age really such "babies"? *Maybe you are* ***judging*** *them* a little too quickly.

My advice is to enjoy your childhood a little while longer; remember, you have the rest of your life to be an adult!

Q. *I have always been pretty even tempered. In fact, my friends all say I'm happy-go-lucky. But lately I've been extremely moody and cranky. What's going on?*

A. Something very normal. The hormonal changes your body experiences during puberty can wreak havoc on your emotions. You feel up, then down—like you're on a

ROLLER COASTER.

Many girls (and boys) feel this way, and it's all part of growing up.

Hormones, however, aren't the only reason you're feeling moody. Your body image is changing, which can be very difficult. You're used to thinking of yourself as a kid; now suddenly you have breasts and curves, and you may feel self-conscious. Maybe for the first time, boys are looking at you in "that" way—or even whistling at you.

Along with a new body comes new feelings, many of which can be confusing.

The boys who used to be pests or *pals* **may now start looking** *cute*. **You might even be in the throes of your first crush. Your feelings toward old girl-friends and FAMILY are** *changing* **too.**

You may find you'd rather meet new friends than hang out with old ones. At school, cliques are forming, and you may feel left out. At home, you want to be alone more. You love your family but need your privacy.

To top it all off, you're probably starting to feel more responsibility for your life. You're beginning to realize that, **EGAD,** some day you will be a grown-up and have to make some serious decisions about your life. And that can be overwhelming!

The good news is, you won't feel this way forever. As you become more comfortable with your new body and feelings and your growing independence, your roller-coaster emotions will even out. Then you will be able to enjoy all the wonderful perks and privileges of growing up. Keep in mind you've got a lot of wonderful firsts—going to a school dance, getting your driver's license, falling in love—all just waiting around the corner for you!

Q. *All of my friends seem to love the fact that they are getting older, but I wish I could stay 11 forever. I am not looking forward to starting my period or having to deal with drugs and alcohol. And boys? Boring! I still like doing kid things, like playing on a swing. Can you help me?*

A. For starters, you may feel better knowing you aren't alone. Even though they may not admit it, many girls (and guys) have mixed emotions about growing up.

Second, keep in mind that you needn't rush yourself. Yes, you are not a baby anymore, but you are still far away from being an adult or even a teen. Eleven is awfully young to have to think about dating. So go ahead and give yourself a few more years before you do. Then, by the time you are 15 or 16, the idea of dating won't seem so scary anymore because you will be old enough to handle it.

As for drugs and alcohol, these are real concerns that unfortunately are affecting kids at younger and younger ages. The best way to steer clear of having to worry about these two big baddies is to hang out with kids who share your values and beliefs. Drugs and alcohol never have to be a part of your life if you don't want them to be. While resisting peer pressure is hard, it's a lot easier to do if you are backed up by friends.

Remember, too, that you *are* still a kid, so it's OK to act like one. So keep on *playing on the swings,* **flying kites,** and **RUNNING IN THE SPRINKLER.** These are activities, by the way, that you should never have to give up, no matter how old you are!

Learn MORE!

Read some fiction books that deal with growing up. You'll feel relieved to learn you're not alone as some of your favorite characters wrestle with many of the same feelings!

A few books to check out:

- *The Long Secret* by Louise Fitzhugh
- *The Summer of the Swans* by Betsy Byars
- *Honestly, Katie John!* by Mary Calhoun
- *Are You There, God? It's Me, Margaret* by Judy Blume

CHAPTER 2

Get This Off Your Chest: All About Breasts

I'll never forget the first time I wore a training bra, when I was in sixth grade. My parents were out of town, and just as I gathered the courage to put it on for the first time, the baby-sitter who was taking care of me walked into the room. "Why, Alison," she exclaimed. "I can't believe it! You're wearing a bra!"

I was so mortified to be "caught in the act" that I ripped the bra off. It took me at least two months before I tried it on again—and kept it on.

Q. At what age can I expect my breasts to start developing?

A. Most girls' **breasts** begin to grow somewhere between the ages of 9 and 14. The process is gradual; it can take up to four or five years before your breasts reach their adult size.

There are five stages of breast development. They were called Tanner stages, after the doctor who first described them. Now they are referred to as sexual maturation ratings (SMR) and correspond to the same Tanner stages.

Stage 1: Before puberty, a girl's breasts are flat except for nipples.

Stage 1

Stage 2: As puberty begins, the tissue under each nipple and the rest of the breast raises slightly, forming breast buds. The nipples also start to grow larger. The **areola**, the circle of skin surrounding each nipple, gets wider and darker.

Stage 2

Stage 3: The breasts and areolas continue growing larger.

Stage 3

Stage 4: Each nipple and areola together form a small, separate mound that sticks out above the rest of the breast.

Stage 4

Stage 5: A girl's breasts grow round and full. The nipples stick out, and the areola is no longer a raised mound on the breast.

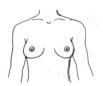

Stage 5

By the way, not all girls go through every stage of breast development. Some go directly from Stage 3 to Stage 5, skipping Stage 4 altogether. Most girls start their period somewhere during Stages 3 or 4.

Q. *Help! My breasts are lopsided! One is smaller than the other. Will my breasts ever look the same?*

A. Most likely, yes. It's common for one breast to develop faster than the other one. In most cases, the smaller breast will eventually catch up with the other one.

But keep in mind that most women's breasts do not match each other perfectly. Most women have one breast that is a little larger than the other. However, this difference is so tiny that no one can usually tell.

Q. *Last week, my breasts started to feel sore and tender to the touch. Yesterday, for example, when I brushed my chest up against the kitchen counter, my breasts hurt. Do you think something is wrong with me?*

A. No. It's normal for girls to experience some soreness while their breasts are growing. After all, your breasts are undergoing a big transformation.

If, however, you are experiencing shooting pains; soreness accompanied by redness, warmth, or sudden swelling of the skin; a lump or hardness in the breast that wasn't there before; or any discharge from the nipple, check with your doctor just to make sure nothing is wrong.

Q. *My sister is five years older than me. My breasts have started to grow, and they don't look anything like hers or my mom's either. Am I OK?*

A. You can relax! **Breasts come in all SHAPES and sizes.** Your breasts may be pointy; your sister's may be round. You may be a B cup; your mom and sister may be a C or D cup.

Keep in mind that there is no one "right" shape, just as there is no one "right" size. So whatever you are, it is the right shape and size for you.

Your weight may also have something to do with your breast size. If you are really thin, your breasts may be on the small side; if you're a little pudgy, fatty tissue can increase the size of your breasts.

Q. *A lot of my friends have nice bust lines, but I'm almost 13 and still flat as a pancake! Does this mean that when my breasts do grow, I'm going to have a small chest?*

A. Absolutely not. Your starting date has nothing to do with how big your breasts are. You may end up having the biggest chest of all your friends. So just try to be patient and wait and see what "develops."

Q. *The other day, I heard a girl talking at school about how she uses exercises to make her breasts bigger. Is this true? If* *so, can you recommend some I can use to make my small chest bigger?*

A. Sad to burst your bubble, but this girl was wrong. Exercise can't increase the size of your bustline for the simple reason that breasts don't have any muscles. So no matter how hard you "work out" your chest area, your breasts are going to stay the same exact size.

FYI, there are, however, muscles on the chest wall just beneath your breasts, called **pectoral** muscles. Developing these muscles may increase the overall size or width of your chest, but it won't make your breasts bigger.

Q. *The other day I noticed a little hair growing around the nipple of my left breast. Is it OK to pluck it out?*

A. No, because this can lead to soreness and infection. It may help to know that lots of girls grow hair on their breasts. As long as you have only a few hairs, there's nothing to worry about. If it really bothers you, however, see your doctor. He or she may be able to recommend a safe way to **remove** the **HAIR.**

Q. *What color are my areolas supposed to be? Mine are pink, but in a picture I saw in a book they were dark. What's normal?*

A. Both. The areola ranges in color from light pink to dark brown. You fall right into this range, so there is no need to worry.

Q. *The other day a friend was over swimming, and as we were changing into our suits I noticed that her nipples stick in instead of out. I'm worried about her. Is she OK?*

A. Your friend is fine. She has what is known as inverted nipples, meaning that her nipples, as you noticed, stick inward. Some women also have flat nipples. The only time a girl (or woman) has to worry about inverted nipples is if a nipple that was not inverted suddenly becomes so. In that case she should see a doctor.

Q. *Some of my friends have started to wear bras. I'm not sure if I need to or not. How can I tell?*

A. If your breasts are starting to feel heavy and uncomfortable, you probably need one. If you don't really need a bra but feel left out because some of your friends are wearing them,

*you can buy a **training** bra,*

a stretchable bra for girls just like you.

Q. *When I hear friends talking about their different bra sizes, I get so confused! It's like some weird math equation or something. What exactly do the numbers and letters mean?*

A. It's simpler than you think. Let's say you are a 32 C. The 32 is how big around your chest is in inches; the C measures your cup size. Cup sizes are measured by letters of the alphabet. An A cup is a relatively small size, a B cup is medium, a C cup is large, and a D cup is for very full, rounded breasts. You can also find AA bras for girls whose breasts are just starting to develop and DD bras for girls with very large breasts.

Q. *The other day, my mom took me to the department store to buy my first bra. I was so embarrassed! The sales lady kept coming in the room to make sure I had the proper fit. Does buying a bra ever get easier?*

A. Rest assured, it does. Once you become more comfortable with the process, the entire experience becomes easier. With practice, you learn what a "good fit" feels like and so no longer need a saleswoman or your mom to help with each and every bra you try on.

Eventually, you will find which size and brand fits you best. Then instead of having to try on several different bras, you can just walk in, quickly buy the bra you know and love, and be gone. It won't be any bigger of a deal than buying a pair of socks!

Q. *I've heard that boys only like girls who have big chests. My breasts have just started to grow, so I don't know how big they'll end up being. But if they turn out small, does that mean guys won't be interested in me?*

A. Luckily, **most guys are a lot SMARTER than to JUDGE girls by the size of their chest.** Sure, some will be attracted to girls with big breasts and maybe even use that as a criterion for dating. But other boys may prefer girls with small breasts.

However, in the end it is how you act, not how you look, that is important. Your personality—*your sense of humor, smarts, kindness, and compassion*—is what will make boys like you, not your bra size!

Q. *Almost overnight, it seems, I've gotten really busty. The other day, a guy I passed on the street whistled and said something about my "knockers." I wanted to die! Why do guys do that, and what should I do if it happens again?*

A. Unfortunately, some guys and men feel it is their right to make comments about girls' and women's bodies. A few do it to harass girls, others, believe it or not, do it because they think you're going to be flattered! Whatever the reason, it is very annoying and a problem women have been dealing with for a very long time.

The best thing to do in this situation is to ignore it. If you confront the guy, he could become hostile or aggressive. This could be dangerous, especially if you are alone or in an isolated place. Hold your head up high and walk on. Remember, he's the one with the problem, not you! Then later, when you are with guys you know and trust, you can discuss some of these issues and enlighten them, if you need to, about how girls really feel when they are treated this way.

Q. *I hear so much about breast cancer. Do I have to worry about giving myself a breast exam?*

A. No. The chance of girls or women under the age of 20 having breast cancer is almost nil. In nearly every case, any lump or irregularity you find at your age is not cancer. Most likely, it can be traced to the fact that your breasts are in the process of growing. They feel "irregular" because you don't know what regular is yet. Also, when you are menstruating, it's common for your breasts to feel lumpy and experience some changes.

That said, if you do find something you think is abnormal or suspicious, check with your doctor just to be safe.

While girls your age don't need to give themselves breast exams, they're usually recommended for women 18 years or older. Because a regular breast exam will be in your future, here's how to do it. There are two parts to a breast self-examination: First you look at the breasts; then you feel them. If during either the visual or manual exam, you feel a lump or abnormal swelling, check with a doctor. Also check with a doctor if your nipples become inverted or leak fluid.

1 GIVING YOURSELF THE ONCE-OVER

Turn on a bright light and step in front of a mirror. Inspect your breasts, looking for any bulge, depression, swelling, patch of rough skin, or change in color.

You should do this in four positions:

✓ Arms relaxed at your sides.

✓ Hands on hips.

✓ Arms raised above your head.

✓ Bending forward.

2 GETTING A "HAND"LE ON THE SITUATION

For the manual exam, first lie down. To examine your left breast, put a pillow under your left shoulder. This will help distribute the breast tissue evenly. Place your left hand behind your head.

Touch your left breast with your right hand. Use the tips of your three middle fingers to feel for lumps or other abnormalities in one of three ways:

✓ You can use a circular motion. Make a large circle around the outside of your breast, moving in increasingly smaller circles to the nipple.

✓ You can use lines. Make vertical lines down your breasts. Start at the armpit and move in to your breastbone.

✓ You can use a "wedge." Imagine your breast is divided like spokes of a wheel, with the nipple in the center. Examine each segment, starting from the out-side of the breast and moving forward, then sliding fingers back to the outside of the breast.

Feel under your left arm for lumps as well. Some breast tissue reaches that far. Then repeat for the right breast. You can also do a breast check in the shower, as shown here.

Q. *How often should women give themselves breast exams?*

A. Once a month. The best time to do this is seven days after the start of their menstrual cycle. If they do the exam before, they may confuse normal swelling of the breasts, due to the hormonal changes brought on by their period, with lumps.

Q. *I know that breasts contain milk ducts so that women can nurse their babies. What else is in them?*

A. Ready for a quickie biology lesson on the breast? Here goes:

Breasts are made up of some 15 to 20 different sections, called **lobes**. Each lobe is surrounded by a layer of fat.

Inside each lobe are structures called **alveoli**. When a woman has a baby, the alveoli produce milk for the baby to drink. The milk travels down the **milk ducts** to the nipple.

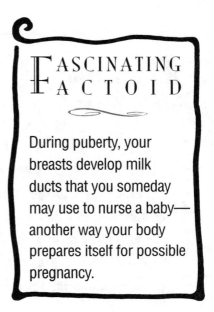

FASCINATING **F**ACTOID

During puberty, your breasts develop milk ducts that you someday may use to nurse a baby—another way your body prepares itself for possible pregnancy.

When a baby sucks on the nipple, milk comes out of the tiny openings in the nipple, which connect with the openings of the milk ducts.

As you begin puberty, you start to develop milk ducts and fatty tissue. These milk ducts and fat are what form your breast buds. The development of milk ducts is one more way your body is readying itself for the time when (and if!) you decide to have a baby.

Breasts also contain nerves, arteries, smaller blood vessels, lymph channels, and connective fibers that give breasts their rounded shape.

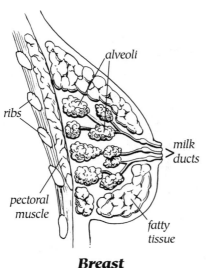

alveoli

ribs

milk ducts

pectoral muscle

fatty tissue

**Breast
(cross section)**

Learn MORE!

You may feel like you're the only girl who has ever had to deal with growing breasts and worry that they're either too big or too small. Talk to your mom, another trusted female relative, or a girlfriend about what you are going through. Ask her how she is feeling or how she felt when she was your age. It's fun to swap stories, plus you'll be amazed at how much better you'll feel knowing you aren't alone.

CHAPTER 3

Other Ch-Ch-Ch-Changes

When I was 11, I began to sweat, and sweat, and sweat, and sweat. After recess I would look under my arms and, to my horror, see two huge wet spots. I couldn't raise my hand in class and kept my arms firmly by my side. When shopping for dresses, I'd give them the "sweat test." I'd put a little spit on the material to see if water showed or not. I'd buy a dress only if it didn't show moisture.

I tried antiperspirants, but they didn't work. Finally, my mom took me to the department store and bought me some sweat guards. These were cotton pads with an elastic band that fit under the arms and supposedly soaked up the sweat so your clothes didn't stain. They were bulky and uncomfortable. Plus, I was worried to death that someone would find out I was wearing them. So, after a few weeks, I threw them away.

Eventually, after the first flush of puberty, I started sweating less. But I continued to give dresses the "sweat test" throughout high school—just in case.

Q. Suddenly, I have shot up to be almost as tall as my mom. I feel like I'm growing an inch a day. Is it normal to be growing so quickly?

A. Yes. Girls usually hit a growth spurt between 10 and 11 that ends at about age 13 or 14. You can expect to grow 3 inches per year for the first 2 years of the growth spurt, then grow only 1 or 2 inches after you start your period. Many girls reach their maximum height around age 15.

By the way, it's also not uncommon for parts of your body to grow more quickly than others. Your hands may suddenly grow, or your feet. But don't worry. **This gawky phase won't last** *forever:* The rest of your body will soon catch up.

Q. *In fifth grade, most of the guys were taller than I was. But now that I'm in sixth grade, I'm the tallest one in the class. Why aren't any of the guys growing?*

A. They will grow soon enough. The answer is that they probably haven't started puberty yet. Girls enter puberty about two years before boys do, so you have a few years growing time on them. In fact, while most girls reach their maximum adult height by about age 15, guys have to wait until they are 19.

Q. *Even though I am eating the same amount as always, I've started to gain weight. Does this mean I need to go on a diet?*

A. Absolutely not. During puberty, not only are you growing taller, you're filling out too.

Suddenly, you've got curves.

Your hips become rounded, and so does your rear. Your face will probably start filling out as well.

While these changes may be disconcerting, keep in mind that it's normal for girls to gain anywhere from 10 to 20 pounds or more during the initial part of their growth spurt. This weight gain is to be expected and means

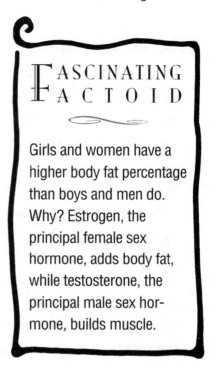

FASCINATING FACTOID

Girls and women have a higher body fat percentage than boys and men do. Why? Estrogen, the principal female sex hormone, adds body fat, while testosterone, the principal male sex hormone, builds muscle.

you are healthy. **It does not mean you need to lose weight.** With time, as you grow used to your new look, you will feel more comfortable with it.

Later in the book, you will learn all about eating disorders, when girls either starve themselves, or eat and then throw up to control their weight. Sometimes girls' eating disorders start at puberty because they misinterpret their body's normal growth as "getting fat." This is very sad because they are not getting fat. They are becoming healthy women. Girls who try to diet excessively to try and stop their bodies from filling out are at risk for many health problems. They also may delay the onset of puberty and menstruation. This is one trap not to get caught up in!

Q. *The other day, my legs were hurting. My mom told me I was having growing pains. Do growing pains really exist?*

A. They sure do! They are pains you may feel in your legs and other parts of the body during puberty. Doctors and researchers don't know exactly what causes growing pains. It may be because your bones are growing a little faster than your muscles, causing aches.

The most common places to feel growing pains are behind your knees, in front of your thighs, and along your shins. You may also feel occasional twinges of pain in your arms, back, groin, or shoulders. Growing pains usually occur late in the day or during the night. They may even awaken you from a deep sleep.

Growing pains can be **an annoying PROBLEM.** You can relieve the hurt by soaking in the tub, applying a warm compress, massaging your limbs, or taking a pain medication such as acetaminophen or ibuprofen. (Before taking any medication, check with your parents.)

If the pains continue or worsen, it's best to see your doctor to make sure they aren't actually a symptom of some serious medical problem.

Q. *I think I've just discovered my first pubic hair. When is the rest of it going to grow in?*

A. The appearance of pubic hair—the coarse, curly hairs that grow around the area between your legs—is another sign of puberty. But just like breast growth, pubic hair doesn't grow overnight. In fact, there are five different stages of pubic hair development:

Stage 1: Before you hit puberty, you have no pubic hair, except for possibly a few fuzzy or downy hairs.

Stage 1

Stage 2: As puberty begins, you grow your first hairs. They are straight and fine, and slightly dark in color.

Stage 2

Stage 3: The pubic hair increases and gets thicker, coarser, and curlier. It also may become darker in color.

Stage 3

Stage 4: The pubic hair continues to get even thicker and curlier and to cover a larger area.

Stage 4

Stage 5: The hair becomes thick, coarse, and tightly curled. It usually grows in an upside-down triangle. Sometimes the hair will continue to grow toward your belly button or down the insides of your thighs.

Stage 5

In general, most girls reach Stage 3 of pubic hair development between the ages of 11 and 13. It is also during Stage 3 or 4 that most girls start their periods.

Keep in mind that just like breasts, girls' pubic hair may look very different. Some women have a lot of it; others have hair that's barely there.

Q. *The hair on my head is red, but my pubic hair is coming in brown. That seems really weird.*

A. Actually it's **NOT AS ODD** as you think. While often the color of the hair on your head will match the color of your hair down there, it won't always. Sometimes the color will be different.

Q. *A friend told me that once I get pubic hair, I have to shower every day to keep it clean. Is this true?*

FASCINATING FACTOID

Pubic hair actually performs an important function. It helps keep the area between the outer lips of your vagina clean. Just like your eyelashes keep dust and other irritating particles from falling into your eyes, pubic hair protects this sensitive area from things that could irritate it.

A. You don't have to bathe or shower every single day. However, you do want to keep the area clean, just like you would the rest of your body. So, when you are showering or bathing, it's important to suds up this area with whatever body soap you use, and rinse well. This is especially important during menstruation, when blood may collect there.

Q. *When can I expect to get hair under my arms? It's not something I am looking forward to!*

A. Most girls start to grow hair under their arms after their breasts begin to develop and they sprout pubic hair. But don't worry, it's not as bad having underarm hair as you may think! If you want, you can shave it. (You'll find shaving tips in Chapter 11.)

Q. *Some of my girlfriends have begun shaving their legs. Do you think that's a good idea?*

A. During puberty, the hair on your legs may become darker and thicker, which may spur some girls on to shave it. The decision to shave or not to shave is a personal one only you can make (and your parents, who probably have strong ideas on the subject). Some girls like the smooth look of a shaved leg; others prefer the NATURAL look.

Q. *The other day I was playing basketball with a friend. After we finished, I smelled under my arms, and I couldn't believe it—I stunk! Is this something I'm going to have to worry about from now on?*

FASCINATING FACTOID

Perspiration is more than 99 percent water.

A. Welcome to another change puberty brings on: **overactive sweat glands.** During puberty, the male sex hormones, or androgens, "turn on" the sweat glands in both boys and girls. Once that happens, the perspiration that collects in body crevices (like your underarms) can lead to body odor.

Luckily, you can arm yourself against a perspiration problem by bathing or showering every day, then applying a deodorant or antiperspirant.

Cool fact

As much as you may hate sweating, your good health depends on it! By wetting our skin, then evaporating, perspiration cools us off and helps our body maintain a healthy internal body temperature. Sweat also helps flush away harmful microbes on the skin.

Q. *Help! I've started to break out. Why is this happening?*

A. Pimples are one unwanted side effect of puberty. And rest assured, you're not alone. Practically every girl or boy who enters this period of life is **bound to BATTLE blemishes.** Some may have only a pimple or two; some endure bad skin for only a couple of years; others suffer from acne even into adulthood.

The reason you're faced with breakouts during puberty is because the oil glands in your skin become more active during this time. Most of these oil-producing glands are located on your face, chest, back, shoulders, and upper arms. This is why these parts of your body can be **"hot spots"** for acne.

The oil glands "pump" their oil into hollow hair shafts (or follicles) that end as little openings, or pores, on the surface of your skin. If these follicles get clogged with oil and excess skin cells, bacteria found on the skin's surface start to accumulate inside the follicle, causing the follicle to become infected. Soon a pimple appears. If the opening of the follicle closes over, a **whitehead** appears. If the follicle remains open, a **blackhead** forms. (By the way, that black dot is not dirt; it is a pigment called melanin, picked up from surrounding skin cells.)

Some people's follicles tend to clog more easily, and they are therefore more prone to developing pimples. Plus, during menstruation, the sweat follicles become more narrow, causing them to clog easier and so increase the chances of getting acne.

If you've been struck with acne, NEVER FEAR! There are many ways to treat it (you can read all about them in Chapter 11).

Q. *I haven't gotten my first pimple yet, but I'm worried they are in my future. Is there any way to tell if you will get acne or not?*

A. There is no surefire way to tell if you'll end up being vexed by your complexion. Heredity, however, does play a role. If your parents had acne, there is a greater chance you will too. In addition, stress can bring on bouts of acne and therefore aggravate a complexion problem.

Q. *A friend of mine has really bad acne. If she touches her face, then touches my hand, let's say, can I get it from her?*

A. You have nothing to fear. Pimples are caused by plugged pores, and that's a condition that is not contagious!

Learn **MORE!**

• During puberty, one of the physical changes you'll notice is
• that you are filling out. If you start feeling critical of your
• new curves, stand in front of the mirror and think of three
• things you *like* about your body.
•
•   Write these things down, and tape your list to the mirror.
• The next time you start to criticize the way you look, instead
• focus on your list. Rather than wasting time feeling bad about
• yourself, you'll start feeling good about yourself!

CHAPTER 4

The "Inside" Story

I was eight or nine years old when my mother first dragged out "the book." She really wasn't ready to fill us in on the facts of life just yet, but my twin sister sure was ready to learn! She'd been bugging Mom for weeks to find out exactly how babies were made. I wasn't so keen on finding out myself, but since I was the youngest (by a whopping 13 minutes!) and didn't want to appear like a 'fraidy cat, I went along with my "older" sister.

Mom opened to the page that showed a picture of the female reproductive organs. As she started to explain, I suddenly felt dizzy and sick to my stomach. I ran to my room and lay down on my bed. About 20 minutes later, my sister came in looking very proud. "You missed something very interesting," she said smugly.

From that day on, I felt a little distance between us. The gulf lessened over the days and weeks, but it took me at least a year to get over that feeling completely.

Q. Am I born with everything inside and outside of me needed to have a baby? Or do these only pop up during puberty?

A. You are born with both external sex organs and internal reproductive organs. During puberty, however, these organs begin to grow and mature.

The external sex organs are those you can see between your legs. The internal reproductive organs are located inside your pelvis. Called reproductive organs because they are involved in creating babies, they consist of the vagina, **cervix, uterus, fallopian tubes,** and ovaries.

Q. *What is the technical term for my vaginal area? A friend of mine tells me it's called the vulva. I've never heard of that.*

A. Your friend is very enlightened. **Vulva** is the clinically correct word for all of the genital organs on the outside of a woman's body.

Here's a quick overview of the different parts of the vulva:

Mons pubis. This is a pad of fat tissue that covers the pubic bone. Pubic hair begins to grow on the mons during puberty. The mons also gets fleshier during puberty and starts to stick out more.

Outer lips (labia majora). The vulva divides into two separate folds of skin, or "lips" (labia). These help protect the area underneath.

During puberty, pubic hair will begin to grow on the outer lips. The lips also become fleshier and may begin to touch each other.

While the outer lips are smooth when you are a child, as you go through puberty, they may wrinkle. They tend to stay that way during most of your adult life.

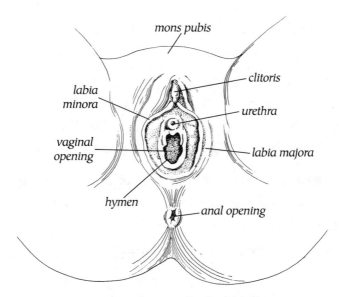

External Female Genitalia

Oil glands on the underside of your body's outer lips (these look and feel like small raised bumps) keep the area moist during (and after) puberty. So you may notice a little wetness that never used to be there.

Inner lips (labia minora). If you were to separate the outer lips, you would find an inner lip at either side of the opening of the vagina.

The skin covering them is pink, smooth, moist, and hairless. During puberty, the inner lips grow, but in general, they remain hidden by the outer lips. Like the outer lips, they may also become more wrinkled.

Clitoris. This is located near the top of the vulva where the inner lips meet. In some women, the lips come together forming the prepuce, a kind of "hood" for the clitoris. The clitoris is very sensitive, and when it is touched, a woman may become sexually aroused.

Vaginal opening. This leads to the vagina, which is inside your body and can't be seen from the outside.

Hymen. The vaginal opening is called the introitus. The outer border of the introitus is a thin layer of skin called the hymen. The hymen itself usually changes in appearance and stretches as you grow.

Urethra. Technically not part of the external female sex organs, this is nonetheless found in the same area. It is the tiny opening just below the clitoris and just above the vaginal opening. Your urine passes through here.

Q. *I know that babies grow inside the uterus, but I don't understand exactly how that works. Does the uterus grow along with the baby, then go back to its normal size once the baby is born?*

A. Exactly. Normally, the uterus, shaped like an upside-down pear, is empty. But during pregnancy, because it holds a growing baby, it expands to many times its normal size.

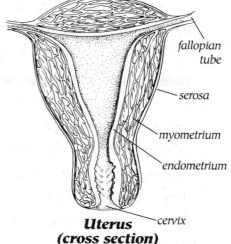

**Uterus
(cross section)**

By the way, the uterus has three layers:

1 The **endometrium**, which lines the inside of the uterus. This lining contains blood vessels (arteries and veins) and secretory glands. These grow and multiply each month to make the inside of the uterus spongy and cushiony.

When a woman is pregnant, the endometrium helps nourish the baby growing inside the uterus. Otherwise, it is shed during menstruation.

2 The **myometrium**, the coat of muscle that contracts during menstruation to expel blood and tissue. During pregnancy, it HELPS PUSH THE BABY OUT. The contractions of this layer of muscle are what cause cramps during some girls' periods.

3 The **serosa**, the smooth outer covering of the uterus.

Q. *Aren't the fallopian tubes attached to the uterus? What exactly do they do?*

A. The two fallopian tubes (or uterine tubes) extend from the top of the uterus but aren't attached to it. The ends of each tube are divided into many tentaclelike structures called **fimbriae**. When you ovulate each month, the fimbriae guide the egg from an ovary into the fallopian tube.

The walls inside the fallopian tubes are lined with tiny hairs called **cilia**. The cilia help to direct an egg from the tube into the uterus. Contraction of the tube also helps move the egg along. The fallopian tubes are very important because this is where an egg is fertilized and pregnancy begins.

Q. *Where do the eggs that are fertilized in a fallopian tube come from?*

A. From the ovaries. Near the end of each fallopian tube is an ovary. One ovary is about the size of a large almond. As you may remember, the ovaries produce the female hormone estrogen, which is responsible for most of the physical changes you go through during puberty.

The ovaries also contain egg cells called ova (a single egg is called an **ovum**). You're born with hundreds of thousands of egg cells. But they don't begin to mature until you start puberty. Once a month, several eggs begin to ripen, but only one (or sometimes more) egg from the ovaries is released into one of the two fallopian tubes.

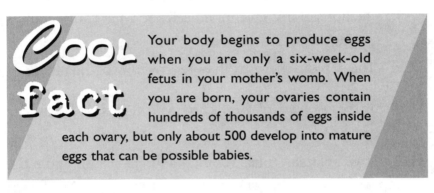

Cool fact

Your body begins to produce eggs when you are only a six-week-old fetus in your mother's womb. When you are born, your ovaries contain hundreds of thousands of eggs inside each ovary, but only about 500 develop into mature eggs that can be possible babies.

Q. *Once I put a finger into my vagina and felt a hard, round knob that feels just like the tip of my nose. What is that?*

A. That is your cervix (by the way, it is perfectly safe to insert a clean finger into your vagina). The cervix is located at the bottom of the uterus and opens into the vagina.

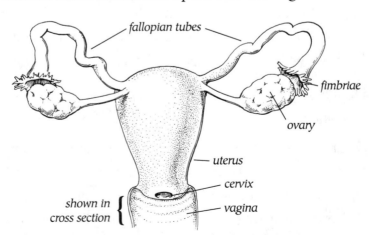

Internal Female Reproductive Organs

Once you start your period, the menstrual flow passes through the cervix into the vagina and out your body. When a woman is pregnant and about to give birth, the cervix stretches wide enough for a baby to pass through.

Q. *The vagina is so small, but I know that during sex a man's penis fits in there. I also know that babies come out of women's vaginas. How does this work?*

A. The vagina, which leads from the vaginal opening to the cervix, is very stretchy. Most of the time it is **like a DEFLATED BALLOON** with all of its inner walls touching. However, during sex the vagina stretches to allow a man's **penis** inside. And during childbirth this small organ expands enough to allow a baby to pass through—even a 10-pounder!

Q. *The other day while getting out of the shower, I took a look at my vaginal area and felt kind of sick to my stomach. Is this reaction really weird?*

A. Not at all. It's **normal to feel a little SQUEAMISH** about this part of your anatomy. The external sex organs can look strange at first and take a while to get used to. Plus, our culture doesn't encourage us to spend a lot of time looking at or talking about our pelvic area. But with time, and as you begin to feel more comfortable with your growing body, you will find that this feeling of discomfort goes away.

Q. *Lately my underpants have been getting wet. Why is this happening?*

A. During puberty, under the influence of hormones, the walls of your vagina begin to shed their cells at a very fast rate, and the vagina produces fluid to wash these cells away. Other cells may also produce a mucousy substance.

Also, if you get sexually excited, the vagina contains glands that lubricate the area.

Q. *The other day when I changed my underwear, there was a yellowish stain on it. Do I have to worry?*

A. No. As you enter puberty, the vagina secretes a clear or milky white, odorless, watery discharge that may stain your underpants yellow. This usually begins to happen several months to a year before the onset of menstruation.

Once you start menstruating, this discharge may change from sticky to stringy and slippery (like egg whites) as you near what's called **ovulation**, your body's monthly release of eggs (you will learn more about this later). Don't worry—it may seem strange, but it's perfectly normal.

Learn**!**
MORE!

● ●

You may have some additional questions about your body and how it works. Go to the library and check out some books on anatomy. The more you learn, the more you will realize how miraculous the human body truly is.

CHAPTER 5

A New You: Starting Your Menstrual Cycle

My twin sister was always the first to do everything in our family. She walked first, she talked first, she was the first to ride her bike without training wheels.

One morning while my family was staying at the beach, I woke up and found a tiny spot of blood on my underpants. When I told my mom, she got really excited. "You're starting your period," she exclaimed. "I can't believe you're doing it before your sister." She rushed downstairs to tell my father and sister the news.

I felt so happy. For once, I had done something first in my family!

Q. *I have one simple question: Why do you get your period?*

A. The female body is designed to conceive and carry children. Your period is a signal that your body is probably able to get pregnant and have a baby. You usually start menstruating one to two years after your body begins to develop, on average between ages 11 and 14. The onset of your period is called **menarche**.

Cool fact

It has been documented that when girls or women live together in the same house, they sometimes start menstruating at or around the same time.

Q. *I just got my first period, and I am so excited! I want to know everything that's going on in my body. How exactly does the menstrual cycle work?*

A. You already learned some of the terms in Chapter 1, but for easy reference, they're included here again.

Every month, the pituitary gland in your brain releases a hormone called the follicle-stimulating hormone (FSH). FSH chemically signals the eggs inside your ovaries to grow.

Each egg, or ovum, is inside its own protective "pod." This is called a follicle (which is how FSH got its name). Every month, one (or sometimes more) of the eggs reaches maturity before the rest. *Once an egg is fully developed,* the pituitary gland receives a signal to release a second hormone called the luteinizing hormone (LH). This hormone causes the egg to be released from the surface of the ovary. This process is called ovulation. The tissue that remains at the site of the empty follicle is called the **corpus luteum**, which is how LH got its name.

A lot of women say they feel more creative right before and during their period. Have you ever felt that way?

At the same time an egg is growing (before ovulation), FSH also causes the ovarian follicle to produce the hormone estrogen. Estrogen prepares the uterus each month for a possible pregnancy. It causes the lining of the uterus to become thick with soft, cushiony tissue and new blood vessels.

Once ovulation occurs, the corpus luteum secretes another hormone, progesterone. Progesterone makes the lining of the uterus even thicker, filling it with larger blood vessels and nutrients, all to protect and feed a developing child.

What happens to the egg once it is released from the ovary? It heads for the uterus by way of one of the two fallopian tubes.

If, while the egg is in the fallopian tube, it meets and joins a **sperm** (a process called **fertilization**), pregnancy begins. The fertilized egg takes a few days to complete its journey to the uterus and settle itself in the uterine lining. During pregnancy, the corpus luteum continues to make progesterone to keep the uterine lining healthy. A hormone from the lining of the pregnant uterus itself stimulates the corpus luteum to keep producing the progesterone.

If an egg is not fertilized by a sperm within 24 to 48 hours after it is released, **the egg will disintegrate.** The corpus luteum will also disintegrate. Estrogen and progesterone levels fall, and the lining of the uterus breaks apart. A mixture of blood and tissue then exits your body through your vagina. When that happens, your menstrual flow, or period, has begun. This entire process is called the **menstrual cycle**.

Soon after your period is over, the whole process begins again, eventually resulting in your next period.

Q. *How long does the menstrual cycle last?*

A. The average length is 28 days. (This means there will be 28 days between your periods.) However, don't be alarmed if your cycle lasts a little shorter or longer. The length of a single cycle can last anywhere from

21 *to* 45 DAYS.

Everyone has a different cycle length.

Q. *My best friend just got her first period, and she had hardly any blood. Is that what I can expect? I hope so, because I have this terrible worry that I will start my period at school, and everyone will laugh at my red pants!*

A. The first time you menstruate, you probably won't leak much blood either. Most girls start with just a few spots of bright red blood or a brown, sticky stain on their underpants.

So, if you are caught unaware without a sanitary pad or tampon that very first time, you may feel a little uncomfortable, but you probably won't have to worry about any blood soaking through your clothes. As a precaution, however, you may want to keep an extra change of clothes in your locker.

If you think your period is coming, consider carrying a supply of pads or tampons in your backpack or purse. If you forget, check with your school nurse. Also, some schools have machines in the bathrooms that sell tampons or pads.

Q. *I've just started my period, and I'm really irregular—I got my period twice in one month. Should I be worried?*

A. Probably not. When you first start your period, it's very normal to be a irregular. You may have your period every two weeks or just once every few months. Once your body gets the hang of the process, which can take a year or even two, you'll no doubt become more regular.

Q. *How long does a period usually last?*

A. Everyone's period is different, but in general, a period lasts between two and seven days. Five days is average. From month to month, the length of the flow may vary.

Q. *Will I have my period my entire life?*

A. If you get pregnant, your period will stop. And one day, it will stop for good when you reach **menopause**, which usually happens when women are between 45 and 55 years old.

Q. *I'm curious. Can you get pregnant before your first period? My friends say you can't, but I think you can. Who's right?*

A. You are. All it takes to get pregnant is for an egg to join with a sperm. And some girls ovulate (release an egg from an ovary) before they get their first period.

While it's much more common for girls to get their period a few times before they actually ovulate, some ovulate right from the beginning. If a girl has sex while she's ovulating, before she has ever had a period, she can get PREGNANT.

Q. *My menstrual flow is really heavy. My sister's is light. Why are we so different?*

A. Because every girl's body is different. Some girls flow heavy, some light. Also, you may start out with a *light flow* and end up with a **heavy flow,** or vice versa. By the way, during your period, you may also pass clots of blood and tissue, which is completely normal.

Q. *How much blood do I actually lose during my period? It sure looks like a lot. If I didn't know better, I'd think I was hemorrhaging.*

A. While it may look like you are losing half your blood supply, rest assured that you are losing only a small amount— at most about a quarter to half a cup. This amount is tiny when compared to your total blood supply.

If, however, you find yourself soaking through four or five sanitary pads or tampons a day, consult a doctor. While there's probably no problem, it's best to get checked out if your flow is extremely heavy.

Q. *My aunt told me that I need to get a lot of rest during my period. She also told me I can't go swimming, because it's not sanitary. Is this true?*

A. A funny thing happens the minute you start your period. You start getting a lot of advice from everyone from relatives to your best girlfriend to the nosy next-door neighbor. While everyone means well, their advice can be as outdated as *your Grandma's taste in clothes.*

Now, about your aunt's "advice":

✳ Nope, it's not true that you have to get a lot of rest during your period. It does not have to interfere with your normal life. In fact, the more active you are, the less likely you are to experience painful menstrual cramps and the better you'll feel.

Sometimes if you are suffering really painful periods, you may have to take time out from your activities to lie down for a half hour or so, but in general, you can be as active as you want.

* It's also not true that you can't swim. In fact, when you have your period, you can swim all you want. Just put in a tampon and dive in! However, you won't want to swim with a sanitary pad on. The pad will immediately absorb the water, not the blood, and you will be lugging around a big soggy mess!

Q. *A friend of mine told me that boys instinctively can tell when you have your period. How embarrassing! Does this mean I can't be around them?*

A. Nope. Your friend is plain old wrong (unless you happen to know any guys who are psychic). **There are no special "HEY, I'VE GOT MY PERIOD" vibes** that a girl sends out.

So relax—your secret is safe. It may help to know that as you get older, it won't seem so important anyway if a guy does know you have your period. You'll start to treat your period as just another normal and very acceptable part of life.

Q. *I've heard I can only take showers during my period because baths aren't sanitary. I'm bummed, because I love to take baths.*

A. This is another false piece of information. There is nothing unclean about taking baths, even if a little bit of blood leaks out while you are soaking. So soak in the tub for as long as you like. In fact, it's a good idea to bathe or shower on days when you have your period so you can keep the area around your external sex organs clean and fight any odor.

Q. *First, my cousin got her period. Then my best friend. Then another friend. Now it seems like almost every girl I know has started menstruating. Do you think I ever will?*

A. Most definitely! Your time will come. Some girls start menstruating as young as 10, others as late as 15 or older.

When you begin menstruating depends on a few different factors:

◆ How old your mother was when she started her period. Most girls menstruate around the same time their mothers did. So if your mom had to wait until she was 15, you may be waiting that long too!

◆ If your breasts have begun to develop. Most girls begin their periods 18 to 24 months after their breasts have started to develop.

◆ How much you eat and exercise. If you are an athlete or very physically active, or if you are dieting and have experienced significant weight loss, your body may put off menstruating. That's because the onset of puberty itself is delayed. Doctors aren't sure why such delays happen. It's possible that a girl simply doesn't yet have enough body fat for puberty (and menarche) to begin.

Q. *Most girls I know can't wait to get their period. I'm the opposite; I'm dreading it. Can you help me?*

A. For starters, it may help to know that such feelings are normal. Your period is a very obvious wake-up call that you are growing up, and you, like most girls, probably have some mixed emotions about leaving your childhood behind.

Some girls also worry that their periods will "hurt." While you may experience a few cramps (which you'll learn more about later on in this chapter), rest assured that the passing of blood through your vagina is painless.

Often the unknown is a lot scarier than reality. I bet that once you actually start your period, you won't mind it as much as you think. For now, you might want to talk to a few friends who have already started their periods. They can reassure you that you have nothing to fear.

Q. *I started my period last year and have been pretty regular. Now, suddenly, I haven't had one in several months. What is going on?*

A. Sounds like you have what's known as secondary **amenorrhea**. This is when a girl has several normal, seemingly regular periods, and then suddenly they stop for three or four months.

This can occur for several reasons:

✳ **Pregnancy.** If you are sexually active and have missed even one period, you should go to the doctor to make sure you aren't pregnant, even if you have only had your period for a few months.

✳ **Stress.** Worries about school, problems at home, or any other long-term tense situation can cause a girl to stop menstruating.

✳ **Extreme weight loss or dieting.**

✳ **Excessive weight gain.**

✳ **Overexercising.**

✳ **Long-term physical illness.**

✳ **Some prescribed medications or illegal drugs.**

✳ **Sudden changes in environment,** like a long trip.

✳ **Hormonal problems.**

If you miss a few periods, it may mean nothing. However, do check with your doctor so he or she can try to pinpoint why they've stopped and make sure that your body is working the way it should.

Q. *My friend just got her period, and she has pretty bad cramps. Do all girls get them?*

A. Many girls and women do experience some cramps during their periods. These cramps can be fairly mild, or they can be very painful. If painful enough, they can sometimes cause a girl to **feel nauseated** and to **throw up.** Sometimes they last an entire period; other times they happen only at the start of the period.

There's no sense in worrying whether or not you will get cramps. After all, you may be one of the lucky ones who either doesn't get them at all or gets them only in tiny doses.

Q. *What causes cramps?*

A. Most experts believe they are caused by hormonelike chemicals in your body that are called **prostaglandins**. Prostaglandins cause the muscles in your uterus to contract during your period. Muscle contractions help the uterus expel the blood and tissue that line it. While these contractions help perform an important function, they can also make you feel pretty darn miserable!

Q. *For the first time last month, I had cramps. I felt terrible! They lasted for two or three days, and one day I felt so bad I had to stay home from school. What can I do to combat cramps if I get them again?*

A. While you may not be able to control cramps completely, there are ways to ease the pain:

✳ *Relax.* It can help to lie down for a half hour with a heating pad (set on low) resting on your lower abdomen. A soothing bath can also make you feel better.

✳ As long as it's OK with your doctor, *take an over-the-counter, aspirin-free pain reliever.* (Ibuprofen and Aleve® are two effective medications available.)

For faster pain relief, take the medication at the first sign of pain. Be sure to take only the dosage prescribed on the back of the bottle.

✳ *Working out.* Mild exercise can help take the pain away. So put on your in-line skates, swat some tennis balls, or take a fast walk around the block. You're almost guaranteed

to feel better getting fresh air and moving around than sitting inside thinking about how rotten you feel!

If none of these remedies helps your cramps, see a doctor. She or he may be able to prescribe stronger medication to ease the pain.

One more thing: Painful periods may be associated with some other, more serious condition. This is another reason to see the doctor if you suffer from severe pain during your period.

Q. *During my period, sometimes I get pains in my legs. Is this normal?*

A. Unfortunately, cramps aren't the only painful part of your period. You may experience any of the following during this time of the month:

✳ Fatigue and lethargy.

✳ Headaches.

✳ Pains in your thighs, back, and groin.

Just in case you are wondering, there is a technical term for all of these symptoms (including cramps). It's called **dysmenorrhea,** or in plain old English, painful periods. As with cramps, light exercise and pain relievers can help clear up these symptoms. (Again, check with your doctor first before taking medication.)

Q. *I've heard my mom and her friends talk about something called PMS. I sure hope I never get it—it sounds pretty bad. What is it exactly?*

A. *PMS* stands for *premenstrual syndrome*. This is a condition where a girl or woman suffers from one or more uncomfortable physical or emotional symptoms a week or two before her period begins. Such symptoms usually disappear on the first or second day of the period. Not all girls and women get PMS, but many do.

If you have PMS, here are some of the symptoms you may experience before each period:

Enlarged, tender breasts

BACKACHES SORE *Headaches*
muscles

Cravings for SALTY or SWEET foods

Abdominal BLOATING

Increased need to urinate CONSTIPATION *WEIGHT GAIN*

Puffy hands or feet

INCREASE or DECREASE in APPETITE *Fatigue*

Mood swings (anxiety, tension, depression)

Whew! That's a long list. But keep in mind that if you develop PMS, it's likely you won't suffer from more than a few of these symptoms at any given time.

Q. *I have the worst PMS! I didn't believe it was real until I got it, but now I know it's real with a capital R. Can you suggest what I can do to feel better?*

A. While there is no surefire "cure" for PMS, there are lots of ways to help ease the discomfort:

Hasta la vista, Babies!

⚙ **Hold the salt.** Salt makes your body retain water. This can cause stomach bloating, puffiness, and weight gain. So say good-bye to foods such as bacon, chips, pretzels, cold cuts, diet sodas, and nuts for the week or two before (and also during) your period.

⚙ **Avoid sugary junk foods,** such as cookies, doughnuts, and cake, a week or two before your period. All that sugar gives you a quick high, but then leaves you feeling more tired than ever. Ironically, some girls and women report that they especially *crave sugary foods* when they have PMS, so if you have these urges, you will have to use extrastrong willpower to fight them!

⚙ **Cut the caffeine.** This means not only coffee and caffeinated teas, but sodas and chocolate too. Caffeine can irritate your stomach as well as make you even more jumpy than you are already feeling.

✪ **Eat three well-balanced, healthful meals a day.** Some girls leave themselves open to premenstrual headaches because, in a futile effort to *stop bloating,* they don't eat enough.

✪ **Exercise regularly.** Working out helps not only cramps, it can fight PMS as well.

If the above suggestions aren't helping, give your doctor a call. He or she may be able to give you further advice or perhaps medication to treat your PMS.

Q. *Which do you think is best to use during my period, tampons or sanitary pads?*

A. It's up to you and what you feel comfortable with. Here's the lowdown on each to help you make your decision:

✧ A sanitary pad is made of layers of soft, absorbent material with adhesive backing that sticks to your underwear.

When you first wear a pad, especially a thick one, it may feel a bit bulky. But you'll get used to the feeling. You also may feel like everyone can tell you're wearing one, but rest assured, they can't. The pads are not visible through your clothes.

✧ A tampon is a rolled cylinder of cotton and other material that you insert into the vagina to absorb the menstrual flow. It has a string attached to the end of it that hangs outside your vagina. When you need to remove the tampon, you simply pull on the string.

You may decide to use only pads or only tampons or, like some girls, use both, depending on what stage of your period you are in.

Q. *Do pads and tampons come in different sizes, or are they one size fits all?*

A. Both sanitary pads and tampons come in many shapes, sizes, and absorbencies. You can find **superthick** sanitary pads for those days when you have a heavy menstrual flow. These are usually called super or maxipads. For light days, or if you have a light flow, you can choose a thin pad or even an ultralight one known as a minipad. For those days when you expect to get your period, you may want to wear a panty shield or liner for just-in-case protection.

Be aware that different brands of pads are shaped and sized differently. One brand's "thin" pad may be slightly thicker than another's. You may want to shop around until you find a product that feels right for you.

Like pads, tampons come in a variety of sizes, from slender for light-flow days to **super** for days when you are flowing heavily. Again, manufacturers size differently, so you might want to test out a few brands before settling on the one for you.

Q. *I feel really stupid asking this question, but I have to know: Can I lose my virginity if I use a tampon?*

A. There is only one way to lose your virginity, and that is to have sexual intercourse for the first time. Your question, however, is a very common one and probably has to do with the hymen, the thin skin that partially covers the vaginal opening.

People used to think that if a girl's hymen was torn or missing, that meant the girl had let a boy put his penis in her vagina. But it might not mean that at all. Some girls are born without a hymen. Others stretch or even tear it by exercising a lot. Tampons may stretch the hymen a bit, but they usually don't tear it.

Q. *The other day I went to the store to buy some tampons but was so embarrassed, I couldn't go through with it. What can I do to get over this?*

A. Lots of girls experience the agony of pulling the box of tampons or pads from the shelf, throwing it casually in her grocery basket (then covering it up with a big box of cereal!), and hoping the checker doesn't notice her strawberry red face while ringing up the purchase.

As embarrassing as all this can be at first, the good news is, it gets a lot easier with practice. Before you know it, buying a box of tampons or pads will be as easy as picking up a carton of milk. And remember, the cashier sells dozens, if not hundreds, of tampons and pads in a day and so doesn't think twice about it.

So next time, force yourself to go through with the purchase. You'll find that the next time after that, the experience will be twice as easy.

Q. *I've just started using sanitary pads, and I have no clue how often to change them. During my last period, I kept changing them every hour, even if there wasn't much blood. Do you think I was overdoing it?*

A. A bit! But that's OK. Normally, you don't have to change your pad any more than every three to four hours.

However, if you flow heavily, you may need to change it more often. Plus, sometimes a pad may smell if you wear it too long. (While menstrual blood is clean and odorless, once it hits the air, it can smell a little.)

When disposing of a pad, do not flush it down the toilet. If you do, the toilet will probably back up and your parents will be stuck calling a plumber. Instead, wrap the pad in toilet paper, and then put it in the trash can. The toilet paper will keep any odor "under wraps."

Q. *I have tried to put in a tampon, but so far I just can't do it. What's the secret?*

A. The main secret is to relax. If you're a little nervous about inserting a tampon, your vaginal muscles may tighten up and make the vaginal opening smaller.

So first, take a deep breath. Now, here is an almost foolproof method for inserting a tampon:

1 Start out with the most slender tampon, as this will be the easiest to insert. Plus, the tampon should come with an applicator, which makes the insertion process easier. Wash your hands thoroughly. Remove the outer wrapping.

2 With your fingers, open both the outer and inner lips covering the vagina, and guide the tampon to the vaginal opening. If the vaginal opening seems dry, try lubricating the area with a little petroleum jelly.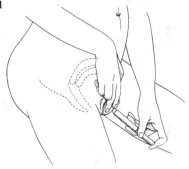

This will help the tampon slide in. (Usually, however, you don't need to do this, because the menstrual blood in the vaginal area will do the lubricating.)

3 Push the end of the tampon with the outer tube (not the end with the string!) into your vagina. Make sure to insert the tampon at a slight angle, as the vagina angles toward the small of the back. Also make sure the tampon goes high enough into your vagina. Otherwise it will feel uncomfortable or even painful—as if it's about to fall out. When a tampon is inserted correctly, you should not feel it at all.

4 Push the inner tube of the applicator into the outer tube. This will push the tampon itself farther into your vagina and out of the applicator. You can then remove the applicator and throw it away in the trash can.

You can insert a tampon either standing, sitting, or lying down. When standing, some girls find the tampon goes in easier if they put one foot up on the toilet.

If you're still having trouble putting in a tampon, you may want to talk to your doctor or to a trusted adult about it. Chances are, you're inserting the tampon incorrectly and just need some practice.

Q. *A friend of mine was over the other day and was showing me how to put in a tampon even though I wasn't having my period. It really hurt! What do you think I'm doing wrong?*

A. You're practicing during the wrong time—wait until you actually have your period. When a tampon is soaked with blood, it glides smoothly into and out of the vagina. But when the tampon is dry, it is painful to push it in and out . . .

o u c h !

Q. *How long can you keep a tampon in?*

A. It's best to change your tampon every three to four hours to make sure you are not "leaking" and to stop any odors from developing. It's not a good idea to leave a tampon in overnight. After using a tampon, read the back of the product box to see if you can flush the tampon down the toilet. Some tampons are flushable; others aren't. If the tampon you're using is not, wrap it in toilet paper and put it in the trash can.

Q. *At camp last summer I heard about a girl who was at a school dance, and her tampon fell out. Could that ever happen to me? I think I would die of embarrassment!*

A. I think someone was pulling your leg. Tampons never just fall out. The muscles inside your vagina hold the tampon firmly in place and prevent it from slipping out. This is one sticky situation you never have to worry about.

Q. *I want to wear tampons, but I'm scared that somehow one might get lost up there and disappear. Can this happen?*

A. It is impossible for a tampon to get "lost." While it fits easily into your vagina, it's too big to go any farther into your body.

TOXIC SHOCK SYNDROME

You've probably heard about **toxic shock syndrome,** otherwise known as TSS. This is a rare disease that has been linked to tampon use. (TSS also can occur in women not using a tampon or not even menstruating. Men can get it too.)

TSS is thought to be caused by a bacterium called **staphylococcus aureus** that lives on the skin and in the body's warm, moist cavities.

Usually, this bacterium doesn't cause problems. However, a blood-soaked tampon is a "nice" environment for this bacterium to grow and multiply and produce a nasty toxin known as TSST-1. This "poison" is believed to cause many of the signs and symptoms of TSS.

Young women under 25, whose bodies may not yet have been exposed to TSST-1, may be less immune to it and therefore more likely to develop toxic shock syndrome.

TSS usually starts out with a sudden high fever, followed by vomiting, diarrhea, light-headedness, achy muscles, headache, red eyes, and a sunburnlike rash, especially on the hands and feet.

If you are using tampons and develop any of these symptoms, see a doctor immediately. If left untreated, TSS can be fatal.

That's because the tampon is blocked by the cervical canal, which is the passageway between the vagina and the uterus. The opening of the cervical canal is no bigger than the head of a match, so it's impossible for a tampon to get through.

Sometimes it may feel like a tampon is "lost" if the string attached to the end of it somehow gets drawn up into the vagina. If that happens, just reach up inside and pull the tampon out with your fingers, careful not to scrape the vaginal walls with your fingernails.

Also, it's possible for a piece of material from the tampon to come off and stay in your vagina. This can lead to infection. If you experience any abnormal discharge (like pus) after tampon use, see your doctor.

*L*earn MORE!

Once you start your period, it's a good idea to keep track of it. That way, you always know when it's coming and can be prepared. Otherwise it may catch you unaware—like when you are wearing white pants!

To keep track, all you need to do is mark down on a calendar the first day of each period and count the days between periods. Once you do this, you will begin to see a pattern, and you can predict when your next period will begin.

For example, let's say there are 30 days between the starting days of your periods. This means you are on a 30-day schedule. You should then be able to look ahead and figure out which day your next period will start.

CHAPTER 6

*L*et's Talk About Sex

I was a late bloomer. Well, let me take that back. Actually, I was an early bloomer—way too early. In third grade, I reached my height of popularity with boys. I had three boyfriends. One of them was the cutest nine-year-old in the entire school. We used to play marbles and tetherball. I think boys liked me because I was the only girl in school who could beat them, and they respected that.

But around sixth grade, I got shy around guys. This lasted pretty much through high school. I didn't even go to my senior prom. A friend asked me, but I wanted to go only with a boy I loved, and I wasn't in love with him, or anyone.

In college, life got a lot better. I met some guys I really liked, and I dated a lot. But I still didn't fall in love. For that reason, I didn't have sex. I wanted to wait until I knew the guy was "Mr. Right." I also wanted him to be in love with me.

That happened in graduate school. I finally met the right guy, and I'm glad I waited. Later on I married him. We just celebrated our 11th wedding anniversary!

Q. When a couple has sex, what exactly goes on? Even though I've had some sex education at school, I'm a bit fuzzy on the details.

A. Here's the scoop: When a man becomes sexually aroused, blood flows into the blood vessels of the penis, and the penis becomes larger and harder. This is known as an **erection**. When a woman becomes sexually excited, her vagina secretes a fluid that makes it easy for the man's penis to slide in. During sex (also called sexual intercourse), a man puts his erect penis into a woman's vagina and moves rhythmically inside her.

The peak of sexual pleasure is called an orgasm. A woman may reach an orgasm one or more times during intercourse. The muscles in her vagina and uterus contract, and her pulse, blood pressure, and breathing rate increase.

When a man reaches orgasm, he ejaculates (discharges) **semen** into the woman's vagina. If one of the sperm in the semen meets and joins with an egg in the woman's body (a process known as fertilization), she will become pregnant.

Q. *How come only one sperm fertilizes an egg?*

A. To answer this question, it will help to explain fertilization in more detail. Here's how it works.

Semen contains millions and millions of sperm. In fact, a normal **ejaculation** produces more than 300 million sperm (that's right—300 million!). These sperm are so tiny that together they could all fit on the head of a pin. After entering a woman's vagina, the sperm have one function: to find the woman's egg, which is resting in one of her fallopian tubes. The first sperm to completely penetrate the egg fertilizes it.

The fertilized egg is called a **zygote**. Once the egg is fertilized, **no other sperm can penetrate it.** The rest of the sperm eventually die off.

The sperm's mission may sound easy, but actually it's very hard. The journey from the vagina to the fallopian tube is a long and difficult one. Some sperm are relatively slow swimmers and simply die of "old age" before reaching their goal (a sperm can stay alive within a woman's body for as long as 48 to 72 hours).

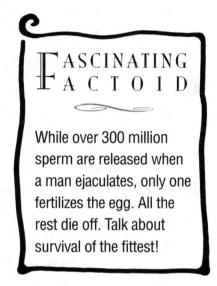

FASCINATING **F**ACTOID

While over 300 million sperm are released when a man ejaculates, only one fertilizes the egg. All the rest die off. Talk about survival of the fittest!

Q. *How does life begin?*

A. Each sperm contains 23 chromosomes, the genetic matter the father contributes to the baby. The woman's egg also has 23 chromosomes, the genetic matter the mother contributes to the baby. When the sperm penetrates the outer covering of the egg and fertilizes it, the 23 chromosomes in the sperm and the 23 in the egg are united.

Life has begun.

Q. *When are you most likely to get pregnant?*

A. Pregnancy is most likely to occur if a girl or woman has unprotected sex a few days before she ovulates (an egg drops into the fallopian tube) or up to two days afterward.

A man can produce the sperm needed to make a baby anytime. But as you know, a woman produces the egg that is needed only once a month.

Q. *I heard some boys at school talking about masturbation. What is this, and is it something only guys do?*

A. Masturbation is when people (boys and girls, men and women) touch their own genitals for sexual pleasure. Some people do it frequently, others not at all. Girls usually masturbate by rubbing their clitoris, boys by stroking their penis until they ejaculate. Masturbation is normal and does not hurt your body in any way.

FASCINATING FACTOID

Each sperm has three parts:

❖ The head, which contains the genetic material the man contributes to making a baby.

❖ The body, or middle section, which connects the head and tail together.

❖ The tail, which propels the sperm forward.

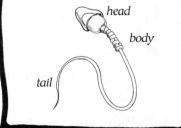

Q. *My best friends are twins. How do twins happen?*

A. There are two types of twins: fraternal and identical. Fraternal twins occur if the mother produces two eggs during ovulation instead of just one. A different sperm fertilizes each egg. Fraternal twins are just as different from each other as any brother or sister.

Identical twins are caused when a single fertilized egg splits into two parts. Two fetuses develop, each containing the exact same genetic makeup. Identical twins are the same sex and look exactly alike.

Q. *I've heard that in high school, everyone is having sex. Is this true?*

A. Of course not. It's just that some kids like to brag about their "conquests." Also, some kids may say they're "doing it" when they're not, in a **misguided attempt to SOUND COOL**.

The American College of Obstetricians and Gynecologists reports that more than 50 percent of females are sexually active by age 17. This means that around half aren't. And the numbers are even less for younger teens.

In fact, today lots of girls (and guys too) are virgins and proud of it.

Teens are finding it saves them a lot of grief and worry to wait until they are older—even until they're married—to become sexually active.

FASCINATING **F**ACTOID

Some research has shown that even if identical twins are separated at birth, they end up having some of the same hobbies and habits. For example, they may both be teachers, play tennis, like the color blue, and even eat lunch at the same time.

Q. *I have a good friend who is older than me who has started having sex with her boyfriend. She isn't using any birth control because she says that since they only have sex occasionally, she doesn't need it. Is this true?*

A. No. Once a girl gets her period, she can become pregnant any time she has unprotected sex. In fact, the majority of teen pregnancies occur within the first six months of intercourse. Actually, most girls do not request contraception until they have been sexually active for six to twelve months. **By then, it may be TOO LATE.**

Q. *My big sister told me that if you jump up and down after having sex, you can't get pregnant because the sperm will fall out. Is she right?*

A. Your sister is wrong. Sperm travel very fast. They're in the cervix within seconds, no matter how many jumping jacks you do. (Please share this information with your sister.)

Q. *If a guy pulls out his penis before ejaculating, can you still get pregnant?*

A. Yes. A small amount of semen is released from the penis even before a boy ejaculates. The sperm could travel into your body, meet with an egg, and *voilà,* **YOU ARE PREGNANT!**

Q. *Can you get pregnant while you are having your period?*

A. Although rare, you *can* have a short cycle and ovulate right on the heels of your last period, so the answer is yes.

Q. *Some of the kids at school have been talking about a drug called Rohypnol. What is it?*

A. Rohypnol is a drug that knocks people out cold. There have been cases when a man has put this or another similar drug into a woman's drink. Then when the woman passes out, the man sexually assaults her.

While very scary, this is something you probably don't have to worry about for now. As you get older and start going to more parties and bars where there is no adult supervision, you will have to be more on guard. Never accept a drink from someone unless you saw the liquid being poured and are sure exactly what is in the glass.

Q. *A girl at our school was the victim of date rape. I'm confused about what date rape actually is. Do you have to be on a date to have it happen to you?*

A. Date rape, also known as acquaintance rape, is when a girl or woman is raped not by a stranger but by someone she knows. The rape may occur on a date but can happen anywhere at any time—like at a party or when a girl is alone with a guy in either of their homes. While date rape is scary to think about, the good news is that you can avoid being a victim by taking a few simple—and smart—precautions:

☛ If you are already dating, **stick to group dates.** Nothing will probably happen if you're with a crowd.

☛ **Hang out with guys your own age.** Older boys are going to be more sexually experienced, and may expect—or demand—more from you.

☛ **Don't let yourself be alone with a guy** unless you know him well and are 100 percent sure you can trust him.

☛ **Avoid being around a boy who has been drinking** or doing drugs. Alcohol and drugs lower people's inhibitions and can cause them to act aggressively and/or irrationally.

☛ **Be clear.** If you are alone with a boy and he starts to touch you in places or ways you don't like—even if he's just holding your hand or hugging you—tell him pronto to stop it and move away from him. Be firm so you do not send any mixed signals that may encourage him. Sure, you risk hurting his feelings, but more important, you save yourself from the possibility he will think you want more than you do and will take advantage of you.

Q. *A friend of mine was sexually abused by an uncle. Does that mean he raped her?*

A. Not necessarily. Sexual abuse is a broad term covering many forms of abuse. Sexual abuse can be physical, emotional, and verbal and can include the following:

☞ Sexual touching or fondling of the child's genitals or the abuser's.

☞ Inappropriate touching on other parts of the body.

☞ Exposing children to adult sexual activity or pornography.

☞ Forcing children to undress.

☞ Acts such as rape or attempted rape.

Sexual assault is a growing problem in our country. It occurs in all racial, ethnic, socioeconomic, and religious backgrounds. It is estimated that 50 to 60 percent of all sexual assaults are committed against adolescents.

Perhaps the most shocking fact of all is that a high percentage of offenders know their victims. Abusers are most likely to be parents, stepparents, relatives, family friends, or caregivers. Fewer than 20 percent of children are abused by strangers, reports the National Resource Center on Child Abuse.

Often kids don't tell anyone they have been abused, because they are afraid no one will believe them or because they are misguidedly ashamed of their actions, even though they did things against their will.

Hopefully, your friend is receiving both medical treatment and counseling for the abuse. If not, she needs to seek professional help as well as notify the police. She also can seek help by calling the local sexual violence crisis center (one should be listed in the phone book).

Q. *I think I might have a crush on one of my girlfriends. I like her a lot. Does this mean I am gay?*

A. No. It's normal for girls (and boys) to feel strong emotions toward their friends of the same sex. Usually, however, these feelings fade and turn to friendship.

If, however, you are feeling continually confused about your sexuality, find someone to talk to, preferably an adult who is in a position to offer you wisdom, support, and guidance.

Q. *Is birth control 100 percent effective?*

A. While many types of birth control have very high success rates at preventing pregnancy, none are successful all the time.

The only effective method that guarantees you'll never get pregnant is abstinence— *not having sex.*

Q. *What kinds of birth control are available?*

A. Hopefully, you are going to wait a long time to become sexually active. But any girl who decides to go all the way with a guy needs to become savvy about birth control.

The following chart describes the most common birth control methods available, including how they work, their pros and cons, and how effective they are.

VAGINAL SPERMICIDE

What is it?: This is a suppository, cream, or jelly that kills sperm. It is placed up into the vagina before intercourse, where it dissolves into a thick liquid that spreads throughout the vaginal area.

Some advantages:
- Easy to buy in drugstores and supermarkets.
- Provides some protection against sexually transmitted diseases.

Some disadvantages:
- Can be messy.
- May irritate the vagina during intercourse.
- Some girls have allergies to spermicide.

Effectiveness: 79 to 97 percent (it is more effective when used with a condom).

CONDOM

What is it?: Also known as a "rubber," a condom is like a tight-fitting balloon that fits over a man's penis and collects the semen when the man ejaculates. Therefore, the sperm is physically blocked from reaching the vagina. Condoms are most effective when used with a spermicide or contraceptive foam to immobilize the sperm. They are made out of either latex, plastic, or animal tissue.

Some advantages:

- Inexpensive and easy to buy in drugstores and supermarkets.
- Can be effective against sexually transmitted diseases.

Some disadvantages:

- Can burst or tear. May have a defect, such as a small hole, allowing semen (and viruses) to leak out.

Effectiveness: 88 to 98 percent (if used correctly and with a spermicide or contraceptive foam).

DIAPHRAGM OR CERVICAL CAP

What is it?: A diaphragm is a shallow latex or rubber cup that fits over the cervix to block the sperm from entering the uterus. A cervical cap, also made of rubber, is smaller and shaped like a thimble to fit over the cervix. Both diaphragms and caps are available through prescription only, and a doctor or another practitioner must fit you for one. They are used with a spermicide, which kills the sperm. To be effective, they must be inserted no more than six hours before and remain in for eight hours after sex. Because the cap can become dislodged, be sure to check its position before and after intercourse.

Some advantages:

- No physical side effects.
- Insertion is easy once you get the hang of it.

Some disadvantages:

- Can be messy.

● Some girls have allergies to spermicide.

● May increase risk of bladder infection.

Effectiveness: 82 to 94 percent (if used correctly).

BIRTH CONTROL PILL

What is it?: This is an oral contraceptive that is taken daily in a monthly series. Combination pills contain hormones to prevent ovulation from occurring. Minipills contain only one hormone and work mainly by thickening the cervical mucus, preventing the sperm from joining with the egg. Birth control pills must be prescribed by a doctor, and one must be taken every day.

Some advantages:

● There is nothing to put in place before intercourse.

● Can help some teens have more regular periods and less cramping.

● Can help facial acne.

Some disadvantages:

● Can forget to take it.

● Can have side effects, such as nausea and weight gain.

● Does not protect you from sexually transmitted diseases.

Effectiveness: 97 to 99.9 percent.

NORPLANT®

What is it?: This is a device consisting of several small capsules a doctor or clinician puts under the skin of your upper arm. The capsules continually release small amounts of progestin. This prevents ovulation and thickens the cervical mucus to keep the sperm from joining the egg. Removal can be done at any time by a doctor or other clinician and should be replaced every five years.

Some advantages:

● Protects against pregnancy for five years.

● No pill to take and nothing to put in place before intercourse.

Some disadvantages:

- Can have side effects, such as irregular periods and nausea.
- Requires a medical procedure to insert and remove.
- Does not protect you from sexually transmitted diseases.
- While not proven, prolonged use of Norplant and other progestin-only implants or injections may decrease bone mass in young women.

Effectiveness: 99 percent.

DEPO-PROVERA®

What is it?: A shot of a hormone is injected into your arm or buttock every 12 weeks. It prevents ovulation and thickens the cervical mucus to keep sperm from joining the egg.

Some advantages:

- Protects against pregnancy for 12 weeks.
- No pill to take and nothing to put in place before intercourse.

Some disadvantages:

- Frequent trips to doctor.
- Can have side effects, such as irregular periods, weight gain, and headaches.
- Does not protect you from sexually transmitted diseases.

Effectiveness: 99 percent.

DON'T FORGET . . . If and when you decide to become sexually active, talk to your doctor to make sure you know all the options available to you. And keep in mind that most of the contraceptives listed above do not provide protection against sexually transmitted diseases. Vaginal spermicides do offer some protection, but latex condoms are the best protection against infection, including HIV, the virus that causes AIDS.

NOT RECOMMENDED FOR TEENS

✳ **The IUD (Intrauterine Device).** This is a small plastic device, inserted into the uterus, that contains either copper or hormones. These cause the uterus to respond in a way that prevents pregnancy.

While the IUD is 97 to 99 percent effective, the uterus of a girl or young woman may be too small to hold it. Plus, IUD users can develop pelvic infections, which may make it hard for them to get pregnant in the future.

✳ **The "natural" or rhythm method.** A woman charts her menstrual cycle to determine when she ovulates (and there-fore is most likely to get preg-

nant), and then makes sure she doesn't have sex during those times. This involves "fertility awareness" techniques, including charting monthly cycles, keeping track of basal body (vaginal) temperatures, and moni-toring cervical mucus changes.

If done correctly, this method is 80 to 99 percent effective. However, it may not work if you have irregu-lar periods, which teens often do. In addition, both partners have to be committed to abstinence during the fertile days. For these reasons, it's not a reliable enough form of birth control for most teens.

Q. *I've heard about something called the morning-after pill. What is it?*

A. This is emergency contraception in pill form that women take after having unprotected sex. This pill, taken within three days of unprotected intercourse, is actually doses of certain birth control pills. It works by preventing the egg from joining with the sperm or by preventing the egg from implanting in the uterus.

The morning-after pill is not a guarantee against pregnancy. However, it can reduce the risk of pregnancy by at least 75 percent. Call your physician if you need information on this.

Q. *What is safe sex?*

A. Safe sex is two different things:

1 Preventing unwanted pregnancy.

2 Protecting against getting a sexually transmitted disease.

Actually, the term *safe sex* is misleading. You can never be completely safe from either pregnancy or disease when you have sex. Check out the chart on birth control on pages 76 to 79 to find out which methods are "safest" for not getting pregnant. The "safest" method for preventing disease is use of latex condoms.

Q. *What are sexually transmitted diseases?*

A. These are diseases you get by having sex with someone who has or carries a sexually transmitted disease (**STD**). For example, AIDS is an STD. Despite breakthroughs in how to prolong people's lives who have AIDS, there still is no cure for this fatal disease.

About one in four Americans has an STD. Teens are at high risk for becoming infected with STDs because they are more likely than other age groups to have multiple partners, to engage in unprotected sex, and for young women, to choose sexual partners older than themselves. In addition, young women are biologically more susceptible to three STDs: chlamydia, gonorrhea, and AIDS.

Here is a quick rundown of common STDs:

❏ ***AIDS (acquired immune deficiency syndrome)*** is the most serious STD because so many people with AIDS have died. AIDS is caused by a virus known as the human immunodeficiency virus (HIV). This virus attacks the body's immune system and leaves the person unable to fight off infections and cancers. An AIDS patient, therefore, is prone to catching all sorts of deadly diseases.

Between 650,000 and 900,000 people in the United States are currently infected with HIV. There is no cure for HIV or AIDS. However, new medicines have been discovered that can slow down the damage HIV causes to the immune system.

HIV is spread through blood, semen, and vaginal fluid. You can therefore get it through sexual intercourse and oral sex. Another risk factor is sharing needles contaminated with the HIV virus. (This generally occurs among drug users. When you go to your doctor's office or the hospital, any needle used on you is brand-new and sterile. A new needle is used on every person, so don't worry!)

The virus can also be passed from an infected mother to her baby during pregnancy or after birth during breastfeeding. **You cannot get AIDS, however, through casual or** *skin-to-skin* **contact. You can't "catch it" by** *hugging, touching,* **or** *breathing* **the same air as an AIDS patient.**

In the past, HIV was spread to people who received infected blood through transfusions. But as of March 1985, all blood supplies are screened for HIV, so there is no longer a risk of catching HIV if you have a blood transfusion.

Researchers are continuing to make advances in their search for a cure for AIDS. But as for now, the disease is fatal.

❑ *Chlamydia.* This is the most commonly reported infectious disease in the United States and may be one of the most dangerous STDs among women today. More than one in ten girls are infected, reports the Centers for Disease Control and Prevention.

While the disease can easily be cured with antibiotics, millions of cases go unrecognized and untreated because chlamydia often does not show any symptoms.

People may pass it on to others without even knowing it!

Once the disease progresses, women may feel itching or burning in the genital area, as well as have a vaginal discharge. Men may find it hard to urinate, and their penis may have a watery discharge.

If left untreated, girls and women can develop pelvic inflammatory diseases (PID), which can cause infertility. Plus, women infected with chlamydia are three to five times more likely to become infected with HIV if exposed.

❏ *Hepatitis B.* This is a highly contagious virus that attacks the liver. In mild cases, you may never know you have it, and it may be gone in six months. But some people become carriers for their entire lives, infecting others along the way.

> Hepatitis B is 100 times more infectious than HIV.

People with hepatitis B may develop cirrhosis, a disease that scars the liver, or liver cancer. There is no cure for the disease, but there is a vaccine to prevent infection.

❏ *Genital herpes.* This is a very common disease that causes painful blisters or open sores anywhere on the genitalia or sometimes in or around the mouth. While the blisters last a few weeks, then go away, the herpes virus does not. It stays in your spinal cord system, and the blisters may come back. While the blisters are present, you are very contagious.

Also, the herpes virus can make you more susceptible to HIV infection and can make HIV-infected individuals more infectious.

Herpes can be treated with prescription drugs to shorten the duration and severity of the symptoms. However, the disease cannot be cured.

❏ *Genital warts.* These are caused by a virus related to the one that causes common warts. Genital warts are hard, painless, **warty-looking** lesions that appear on the sex organs or around the anus.

Doctors either prescribe a cream or lotion to get rid of them, or they may freeze them off or laser them. If the warts are large enough, they may have to be surgically removed. Even after they are treated, they may come back.

❑ **Gonorrhea.** While gonorrhea has declined since the mid-1970s, rates of infection remain high among teens and young adults. Gonorrhea often doesn't show any symptoms. If symptoms do appear, a woman may experience vaginal discharge, pain while urinating, and bleeding between monthly periods.

Gonorrhea can be treated with antibiotics. If left untreated, however, it can cause PID and sterility.

DO YOU KNOW WHAT'S REALLY SCARY ABOUT STDs?

✗ Anyone who has sex is at risk.

✗ Sometimes the symptoms don't show up for months (if ever). You can't tell you are sick, so you don't get treatment. Plus, you may be spreading the disease without even knowing it.

✗ You can get more than one STD at the same time from the same person.

✗ STDs affect the health of women more severely than men. They can make a woman infertile and have been linked to cervical cancer.

✗ They can kill you.

If you think you or someone you know has an STD, **contact the Centers for Disease Control and Prevention's National STD Hotline** at (800) 227-8922. This hotline provides basic information about the diseases and can refer you to a local public health clinic.

❏ *Syphilis.* Syphilis has declined greatly in recent decades. However, an estimated 70,000 cases are diagnosed each year in the United States.

People with syphilis develop painless sores on their genitalia or mouth. The disease can be treated with antibiotics. If left untreated, however, it can lead to heart diseases, brain damage, blindness, and even death.

❏ *Trichomoniasis.* This is a common cause of **vaginitis** (irritation or inflammation of the vagina). Women with this disease usually suffer from vaginal itching, pain while urinating, and vaginal discharge. The good news is, it can be treated with antibiotics.

Learn MORE!

Spend some time thinking about your values and priorities regarding sex. What are some good reasons for waiting to become sexually active? How will you handle possible situations where you are being pressured to go farther than you want? You may also want to discuss these topics with friends. It's always fun—and informational—to brainstorm with your pals about an important topic like this one.

SAFE CONDOM USE

A condom is your best bet against acquiring AIDS or another STD—but only if used correctly. Here is the right way to use a condom:

✓ **Only use a latex condom.** Plastic condoms do not necessarily protect you against infection.

✓ **Use a condom** each and every time you have sex.

✓ For extra protection, the woman should **put spermicidal foam, gel, or suppositories** in her vagina. This will help prevent STDs and pregnancy.

✓ **Treat condoms gently** so they don't get damaged.

✓ **The condom should be placed over the tip of the penis, lubricated side out, and then rolled downward toward the base of the penis.** A half inch of space should be left in the tip of the condom to hold the semen. A tight-fitting condom is more likely to tear.

✓ After sex, **the penis should be withdrawn immediately** to prevent the condom from slipping off as the penis loses the erection.

✓ **Use a new condom** if you have sex again.

CHAPTER 7

*L*et's Hear It for the Boys

When I was 13, I went to tennis camp. There I fell head over heels for one of the counselors. His name was Doug, and he must have been about 18 or 19.

One night I was wearing a yellow shirt and brown pants. "You look really pretty in that outfit," Doug told me.

Well, as you can imagine, I was jazzed. So the next night I wore the same outfit . . . and the next . . . and the next. I must have worn it 10 times in 20 days. By the time I got home I was so sick of that yellow top and brown pants, I practically threw them in the trash. But you know what? While I wore them, I sure felt fabulous.

Q. *OK. So I know boys have a penis. But there must be more to a boy's body that helps him make babies. How does it work?*

A. A male's external sexual organs consist of a penis and a **scrotum**.

The penis is made up of mostly spongy tissue with many large blood vessels running through it. The scrotum is the sack of skin that hangs down behind the penis and holds a male's **testicles**.

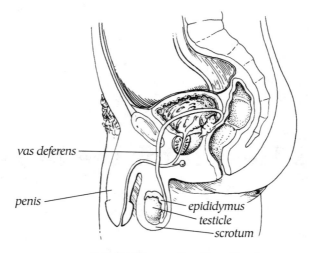

Male Reproductive System
(cross section)

The testicles are two small egg-shaped organs, one inside each compartment of the scrotum. The left scrotum usually hangs lower than the right. The testicles are where sperm are made. These organs also contain cells that secrete the male sex hormone, **testosterone**. This is the hormone responsible for most of the sexual changes that occur in boys during puberty.

Q. *How and why do boys get erections?*

A. Normally, the penis hangs loose. However, when a man becomes sexually excited, the blood vessels inside the penis fill with blood. The penis swells, getting hard and erect.

Boys have erections from the time they're born. **Even baby boys have them!**

However, when a boy enters puberty, erections happen more often. A boy can have one just thinking about kissing and making out or by just looking at a girl. He can also get them when he's not thinking about sex at all or have an erection in his sleep. An erection goes away either by itself or through an ejaculation, when the penis releases semen.

Q. *What is semen made up of and where does it come from?*

A. Semen is made up mostly of sperm cells transported in a mucous liquid. Semen comes out of the tip of the penis. Both urine and semen pass through the same opening, but not at the same time.

FASCINATING FACTOID

The testicles, where the sperm are produced, lie outside a boy's body because sperm need a cooler-than-normal body temperature to survive.

Sperm cells are produced in the testicles. They pass from each testicle into the **epididymis,** the half-moon shaped structure that sits directly on top of each testicle inside the scrotum. The sperm mature and are stored in the epididymis, where they are mixed with a mucous substance until they are emitted.

The **vas deferens** is a thin tube that carries the sperm from the epididymis down to the ejaculatory duct. The ejaculatory duct is located inside the boy's body in the pelvic area. This duct receives not only the sperm but also more fluid from a special gland called the seminal vesicle.

Once the sperm are mixed with this fluid, the semen is propelled into the urethra (a hollow tube that runs from the bladder, then along the entire length of the penis) and, finally, out of the penile opening during ejaculation.

Q. *Does a boy's body go through several stages of development during puberty just like a girl's body?*

A. Yes, it certainly does. In general, boys start and finish puberty later than girls. Along the way, here are the changes they go through:

Stage 1: Before puberty there is no pubic hair and no growth of the external sex organs.

Stage 2: Puberty begins when the pituitary gland and hypothalamus in the brain start producing hormones that trigger the testicles to begin producing testosterone and other male hormones. The testicles, scrotum, and penis begin to enlarge. This usually begins when a boy is between 11 and 16.

Stage 3: A boy's pubic hair begins to grow around the base of the penis. His testicles and scrotum continue to grow, and he often has his first ejaculation. In addition, a boy's voice deepens.

Stage 4: The testicles and penis continue to grow. The pubic hair becomes darker, coarser, and curlier. The boy begins to grow underarm and facial hair and experiences a growth spurt.

Stage 5: The boy is now physically an adult. He has reached his full height, his sex organs have reached their full size, and he has developed his deepest voice. His body hair distribution is that of an adult, with pubic hair on the inner thighs and extending upward onto his abdomen.

Q. *I'm really confused. A guy I like a lot is pressuring me to go all the way with him. I don't want to, but I don't want to lose him. Help!*

A. First of all, **YOU'RE SMART TO WAIT TO HAVE SEX UNTIL YOU ARE OLDER** for several reasons:

❀ You don't have to worry about getting pregnant or catching a sexually transmitted disease.

❀ Girls your age aren't really prepared for the big-time emotions that go along with being sexually active. (For example, girls tend to get overly attached to boys they have sex with, even if the guy isn't really for them.)

❀ Sex is much more fulfilling when you love someone and have a committed relationship, like marriage.

Now, about this guy: It's better to lose the relationship than lose your virginity. Besides, if this boy really cares about you, he'll respect your wishes. While in **the short run** it may be hard to say good-bye to him, in **the long run** you will be better off.

Q. *I'm only 13, and I had sex with a boy. Now I wish I hadn't. Luckily, I'm not pregnant, but I'm feeling mad at myself and guilty.*

A. You can't erase what you've done, but you can learn from it. And it sounds like you've learned a valuable lesson: that you want to wait a while until you become sexually active again. Try focusing on what you have gained from your experience *(wisdom!)*, and you may stop beating yourself up so much.

Right now you need to talk to someone you really trust, preferably an adult. Once you get your feelings off your chest, you'll discover they don't weigh down on you so much. Your trusted adult also may be able to give you some advice on how not to get yourself into this situation again.

Q. *I've heard that as you get older, guys really start pressuring you for sex. Is this what I have to look forward to?*

A. For the record, not all guys will put the squeeze on you to "go all the way." There are **plenty of boys out there who wouldn't dream of PRESSURING a girl** into doing something she does not feel comfortable with.

Some boys, however, may push girls to go farther than the girls want. Chalk it up to the surge in hormones teenage boys experience, as well as the pressure *they* may receive from *their* friends to be sexually active. While girls also have sexual feelings and desires, they often tend to view kissing and making out as a way to get emotionally close to a guy. Some boys, on the other hand, may view them as ways to get sexually close to a girl.

Sometimes guys use lines to get a girl to say yes. These might be:

> **"I'll break up with you if you don't."**
>
> "You've been **leading me on**."
>
> *"You have to finish something you started."*
>
> **"Everyone's doing it, so why shouldn't we?"**
>
> *"We love each other, so it's OK."*

If a guy uses these lines or other ones on you, remember that they are just things a guy might say when he wants you to cave in to his pressure. Stay true to your heart and wait for that guy who will wait for you!

Q. *Lately, I've started to notice boys. And ever since, I can barely squeak out a word when I am around them. What can I do about this?*

A. Lots of girls find themselves suddenly shy around guys. After all, you're looking at them completely differently. It used to be that boys were only good for teasing or batting baseballs with. Now, suddenly, you feel like batting your eyes at them!

The next time you find yourself growing tongue-tied around a guy, here are some suggestions:

♥ Remember that yes, he is a member of the opposite sex, but first, he's a human being. By *thinking of guys as people,* not boys with a **capital B,** you may cut down some of your anxiety.

♥ Keep in mind that any guy you talk to is probably **just as NERVOUS** as you are. After all, he's entering puberty, too, and experiencing many of the same feelings that you are.

♥ GET TO KNOW GUYS THROUGH ACTIVITIES. Let's say you join the environment club. You'll feel a lot more at ease talking to guys if there is a reason to do so—such as discussing how to save trees. Plus, if you are out doing something together—making posters or planning an event—you'll be so caught up in your mutual activity that you won't have time to even think about feeling nervous.

♥ If you are going to be one-on-one with a guy in a social setting, **COME PREPARED** with a few preplanned things to talk about, such as a paper you're both writing or the big game that's coming up that weekend. By having a few safe topics ready to bring up, you'll never have to worry about being speechless!

Q. *I've been dating a boy for a few months, and now he says he wants to go steady. I'm not sure I want to. What do you think?*

A. At your age, it's best not to rush into a relationship, even if you and the guy really care about each other. While you may feel like a grown-up—especially with a new grown-up body—chances are, you're not emotionally ready for a heavy-duty relationship.

Tell the boy you are just not ready to "settle down." He may be disappointed, but a part of him may also be relieved. Deep inside, he's probably not ready either. Remember, both of you have your entire lives to meet and date members of the opposite sex, so take it slowly.

Q. *Last week I liked one boy. This week I like another. It's exhausting! Will I always be feeling so fickle?*

A. For a while, you can expect your affections to swing wildly from this guy to that. Now that you've discovered boys, it's hard to choose which one you like best. They're all so cute and nice!

While you're in this phase, just make sure you don't take your **"flavor of the week"** too seriously. Maybe the guy you're crazy about on Monday doesn't talk to you. Don't get upset, because by Friday you may not even care. If you can, try not to take your feelings too seriously until they settle on one guy for a longer period of time.

Q. *Last month I met this absolutely adorable guy. He's funny, nice, and smart. Whenever I'm with him, I have the best time. I think I'm in love. My parents say I'm too young. Do you?*

A. Love is a very intense, complex emotion. It's sometimes even hard for adults to know if they are in love with someone or merely infatuated. Usually, time is the telling factor.

Infatuations are short-lived and intense. They usually involve physical symptoms, like a fast heart rate or giddiness when you are around the guy you like. They tend to burn out once you really get to know the guy. Who he *really* is just doesn't match your grand illusions!

Love, on the other hand, grows stronger over time. The more you get to know the guy, the more you appreciate him. People in love usually share common interests, beliefs, and an attitude on life.

> LOVE ALSO MEANS TRUSTING SOMEONE 100 PERCENT AND BEING COMMITTED TO HIM.

Now that you know a little bit more about love, you can decide if what you are feeling is the real thing.

Q. *I have a huge crush on Leonardo DiCaprio. I think about him all the time. My sister says I'm wasting my time. Am I?*

A. Crushes do take up a lot of time and energy. And chances are, you'll never be Mrs. DiCaprio.

On the other hand, crushes at your age are completely normal. Being infatuated with guys way out of their reach, such as movie stars or rock stars, is a harmless way for girls to explore their new-found attraction for the opposite sex.

Just remember that a crush is just that—a crush. By definition, it is a one-ticket ride to romance. While it's OK to drool over your Leo poster now and then, don't let your feelings for a superstar you'll never meet be a substitute for the real thing.

Q. *I was dating a guy for a while, but we broke up. I'm miserable. Will I ever get over him?*

A. There is nothing tougher than breaking up with a guy you've really cared about. You may daydream constantly about all the fun things you did together. You may also feel like you never want to date anyone else again.

While it may seem like you will always be feeling this way, rest assured, you won't! Yes, you will feel sad for a few days, weeks, or maybe even months. Slowly but surely, however, you will discover that you aren't thinking about your ex as much. Then one day you'll look at another guy and think, "**GEE, IS HE CUTE!**" When that happens, you know you're almost cured.

Q. *My best friend is a boy. I know people call me weird behind my back. Am I?*

A. Not at all. Many girls have good friends who are boys. The only time it can get a little dicey having a boy as your best friend is if—and I said if—one of you starts to develop romantic feelings for the other. Then someone is bound to get hurt.

BUT PURE FRIENDSHIPS BETWEEN BOYS AND GIRLS CAN AND DO EXIST.

By the way, are you sure everyone thinks you are weird? I bet if you asked them, you'd be pleasantly surprised to discover they think your friendship is terrific.

Q. *I really like this guy and I think he likes me, but I'm not so sure. My friends say he is, but they might just be saying that to make me feel good. How can you tell if a boy is interested?*

A. There is no exact science to determine if a guy likes you or not. However, here are a few questions to ask yourself that may tip you off as to whether the answer is yes:

➜ Does he make a special effort to talk to you? For example, if you're halfway across the cafeteria, does he walk over to say hello?

➜ Does he take an interest in you, meaning, does he ask you questions and/or make comments about what you are doing or how you look?

➜ Does he try to get close to you? If a group of you are at lunch, does he somehow manage to sit right next to you?

➜ Does he make excuses to get together, using lines like, "*Want to come over and see my kid brother's* **worm** *collection? You know, my brother really likes you, and it would be important to him."*

All these behaviors signal that he has feelings for you. In fact, I'd say he's head over heels about you!

Q. *There are a few boys at school who want to date me. My mom says I can only go on group dates until I'm 15 or 16. I'm 13, and that seems like a long way off. What do you think?*

A. Call me old-fashioned, but I'm with your mom. Here's why: If you start dating, that means you're going to be spending a lot of one-on-one time alone with guys. While this sounds great, it might end up making you uncomfortable. What if you get stuck on a date with a guy you don't really like, but he's obviously smitten with you? It can be awkward. Or maybe you and the guy don't click at all, and you'd rather be home watching the History Channel. Or, most important, if you're alone with a boy, the greater the chances are he may try to pressure you into going farther physically than you want to.

However, if you're with a group, you can still talk one-on-one with a guy but without the pressure. If a conversation goes sour, no problem, you're not stuck. Just talk to another boy in the group. While dating seems like freedom, at your age, actually it can be more free—and more fun—in a crowd.

Save the one-on-one dating for when you are older.

Q. *I am good friends with this boy and may even be interested in him. He lives on the other side of town, and I hardly ever run into him except at my brother's soccer games, because they are on the same team. I want to call him and invite him to come to my family's barbecue, but a friend of mine told me a girl should never ask a boy out. What do you think?*

A. I think **it's perfectly fine to ask a guy out.** In fact, many boys like it when girls take the initiative because it takes the pressure off them. So what are you waiting for?

Learn MORE!

What type of guy do you dream about? Is he tall? Does he have blond hair? Brown eyes?

While looks are important, spend a few minutes thinking of some of the inner qualities you want in a boy, such as a sense of humor, kind nature, and so on. This will help point you in the direction of boys who are your type, as well as get you to see beyond a guy's appearance.

CHAPTER 8

𝓕riendships, Feelings, and Parent Problems

*I*n sixth grade, a new girl moved to our school. Her name was Cristi, and we became best friends. Then in seventh grade, when we went to junior high, she dumped me for a "cooler crowd." I was devastated but made new friends.

Then, during the first week of high school, Cristi walked up to the table where my sister and I were eating lunch. "Can I sit with you?" she asked. We hesitated for a moment, then said "Sure." Turns out, the crowd she'd hung out with were getting into drugs, and Cristi didn't want to be any part of it. At first I was hesitant to take her back as a friend because I worried she'd drift back to her old crowd. But as the weeks rolled by, I realized the friendship was going to last.

And it did. Today, Cristi is still my best friend.

Q. Help! I used to feel I was friends with just about everyone. Now, suddenly, cliques have formed, and I feel left out. What's going on?

A. Once you reach the sixth or seventh grade, something strange happens. Girls develop a "pack" mentality and start hanging out in groups. They tend to dress alike, talk alike, and wear identical hairstyles. And they aren't always friendly to people outside their group.

Girls form cliques out of a need to fit in. **Often girls who act the most snobbish are actually the most insecure.** They want to be popular and are desperate to "make it" on the social scene. So they pick a few friends to surround themselves with so they never feel alone.

It sounds like you are used to having many friends and probably still do, even if the girls have joined cliques. Try to separate your old pals from the rest of the pack and do activities with them individually, like going for a bike ride or baking cookies. One-on-one, you can talk to them and reestablish the relationship.

To make new friends, join a club or get involved in a new activity, like tennis. It's easier to become pals with kids who share a mutual interest.

Q. *I am a member of a clique. While it's great to have a crowd of friends, sometimes I feel like I'm suffocating. How can I branch out without losing my friends?*

A. By being yourself and being friends with whoever you want. If the girls in your clique are true friends, they'll stand by you. And if they don't, they weren't really friends to begin with, so you are better off without them.

If you want to be buddies with kids your clique deems "nerdy," go ahead and do so. Keep up with old friends, even if they're in another clique. Only by staying true to yourself will you feel good about yourself, no matter what the clique says.

Besides, if you branch out, you may give the other girls in the clique the chance to make new friends too. If you're feeling suffocated, chances are, you're not alone.

Q. *I like to wear funky vintage clothes and have really short hair. But all the girls at school wear sweater sets and jeans, and have long, straight hair. I feel pressured to start dressing like them and let my hair grow, even though I don't really want to. But if I don't, I may never fit in. In fact, some of the kids tease me a lot, especially because of the clothes I wear. What should I do?*

A. If you're really unhappy with the way you're being treated, you could make a few concessions to the popular style. As long as your parents are willing, why not buy one or two outfits that are more in line with those of your peers? **BUT DON'T CHANGE YOUR ENTIRE WARDROBE.** In junior high school, kids who dress like the other kids are generally more accepted. However, the truth is, kids your age can find *many* things to tease each other about. **SO DON'T CHANGE YOUR PERSONALITY OR ANY-THING ELSE YOU REALLY CARE ABOUT,** like your hair. In the end, it's much more important that you're confident, and comfortable with yourself.

Q. *One of my friends is really popular. Everyone seems to like her. I think it's because she is a good listener—I know that's why I like her. How can I be a better listener?*

A. Easy. Just follow these tips:

* ✳ **Ask questions** of the other person, such as, "Are you having fun on the soccer team?"

✳ **Really listen** to his or her answers (instead of thinking about how *you'll* reply), and ask a follow-up question.

✳ **Don't interrupt.** This makes people feel like you aren't interested in what they have to say.

✳ **Nod your head** and say "uh-huh" when people are talking so they're assured you're following them.

✳ After someone is done telling you something, **sum up what was said** in a sentence or two ("sounds like you're feeling frustrated") so the other person feels she's being understood.

Soon, with a little practice, being a good listener will become second nature to you. Now let's just hope some of your friends also take this advice, or you'll never get to talk anymore!

Q. *I have had the same two best friends since kindergarten. Now, suddenly, we're growing apart. I don't know what to do. Can you help?*

A. As painful as it is, this is all part of growing up. One reason you may be drifting away from your old friends is that you were thrown together out of convenience, not choice. For example, maybe the person who's been your best friend lives next door to

you. Over the years it was easy to become good buddies for the simple reason that you lived so close together. But now that both of you are older and at the age where you are consciously choosing your friends, you might be discovering you don't have that much in common.

Other times, girls may feel they need a change and may be attracted to new friends simply because they are new. In this case, often after the first flush of the relationship wears off, girls discover they don't really click with their new pals and turn back to their tried-and-true friends.

The bottom line is, you and your friends may stick together after a few rough patches, or this may signal the end of the friendships as you've known them. If you are finding that your best efforts to hold friendships together aren't working, there's not much you can do. But be cheered that in many instances, you and your friends will come back together.

Q. *I am having a terrible time because all the girls I hang out with talk about people behind their back. For example, after a girl leaves the room, they say mean things about her. I hate this, plus I wonder what they say about me when I'm not around. What should I do?*

A. While you can't change the way the other girls behave, you can control your own actions. **Make it a rule that you will never cut anyone down.** When the other girls start doing it, tell them firmly how you feel. You may be nervous about doing this because you think they won't like you anymore. However, what you'll probably discover is, they will respect you.

You also may find that other girls in the group feel the same way. Once you step forward to stop the backbiting, they may back you up. If, however, nothing changes, you may want to consider looking for some new friends.

Q. *I have this really good friend, but she does something that drives me crazy! One day she's really nice to me at school. The next day she ignores me. I never know if she's going to be friendly or blow me off. What should I do?*

A. First of all, I don't think this girl qualifies as a "really good friend." **IT SOUNDS LIKE SHE IS USING YOU.** She knows you'll be there if she's feeling down or lonely but doesn't think twice about ignoring you if there are other kids she'd rather talk to.

It's worth a try to talk to her and point out that you feel hurt by her actions. However, she may not change. Your best bet then is to remain friendly to her (there's no need to get revenge by acting hot, then cold, just like her), but don't rely on her as a friend. A real friend is someone who is consistently nice and friendly to you. Cultivate friendships with girls who treat you thoughtfully this way.

Q. *I lied to my best friend and feel so guilty. What should I do?*

A. For better or for worse, most of us lie to our friends at some point in the relationship. However, that doesn't make it right. So why not tell your friend the truth? Explain to her why you lied, and ASK HER FORGIVENESS. Chances are, as long as you present your explanation in a caring way, she will forgive you. Then next time you are tempted to lie, remember how bad it felt and resist the urge.

Q. *Sometimes I get really down. I am in a good mood, then something happens, and my mood crashes. What can I do to feel better?*

A. Sometimes a little depression and sadness is part and parcel of puberty. This time of your life is one of great disappointments as well as great expectations. You look forward to seeing the guy you like at school, and then he ignores you. You spend weeks waiting for the school dance, then when you get there, you feel awkward because you don't like the outfit you bought and want to go home. Adolescence is a time of heightened emotions as well as new experiences you're not sure how to handle.

You may take out your frustrations on others or even yourself. You may beat yourself up with thoughts like you're no good, you're not nice enough, or how could anyone like you?

You can begin to cope with these overwhelming emotions by

✦ **GETTING THEM OFF YOUR CHEST.** Talk to a close friend about them or express your feelings in a journal or a song.

✦ **GETTING REGULAR EXERCISE. Aerobic** workouts—running, walking fast, dancing, cycling—have been proven to boost people's moods.

✦ **BLOCKING OUT SOME PRIVATE TIME EACH DAY.** Let this time be just for yourself—time to do whatever you want, even if it's just hanging out with your cat.

✦ **ACCEPTING YOURSELF.** It's OK to feel lonely and think no one understands you. Everyone feels that way sometimes. Just ask your friends!

✦ **LOOKING FORWARD TO THE FUTURE.** As you continue to grow up and learn more about yourself, chances are, the depression will go away. You'll feel more confident about yourself—who you are and where you fit in.

WARNING SIGNS OF DEPRESSION

Sometimes if you feel really down, you need to get professional help. Here are some symptoms of a big-time depression to watch for:

➤ You've been feeling constantly down for weeks or even months.

➤ You aren't interested in anything, even the things you used to love to do.

➤ You're sleeping a lot and sometimes can't get out of bed.

➤ You've gained or lost weight.

➤ You can't concentrate.

➤ You're avoiding family and friends and are feeling isolated.

➤ You put yourself down a lot.

➤ You think you'd be better off dead.

If you are suffering from these symptoms, there are many people who can help you:

➡ **Your parents.** They can give you reassurance and comfort. They also may suggest you see your family doctor just to make sure there is nothing physiologic contributing to your depression.

➡ **School counselors.** A school counselor is there to help you not only with academic issues but emotional ones as well. Go to him or her and explain how you're feeling. Just talking to the counselor may help you feel a lot better. Or the counselor may refer you to another professional, such as a psychologist or psychiatrist.

➡ **Psychologists.** Men and women trained and licensed as psychologists offer many techniques and methods to help alleviate depression. Some schools have a staff psychologist on campus. Or you may need to talk to your parents about finding a private psychologist.

➡ **Psychiatrists.** These professionals have a medical degree and, in addition to giving advice and comfort, are licensed to prescribe drugs for mental disorders.

➡ **Social workers and marriage and family counselors.** These mental health workers hold master's degrees in either social work or psychology.

➡ **Clergymen or women.** The minister, rabbi, reverend, or priest of your church or synagogue can provide counseling and a spiritual approach to treatment.

Remember, no matter how down you are feeling, you never have to face these overwhelming emotions alone.

Q. *I have a friend who talks about killing herself. Should I take her seriously?*

A. Yes, you should. **Suicide is a BIG problem among teens.** When caught up in a black mood, teenagers sometimes mistakenly believe that life isn't worth living. They may feel no one cares about them, and that nothing will ever improve. But suicide is a terrible permanent solution to a temporary problem.

Sometimes kids take their lives with a gun or jump off a cliff. Other times, they try to kill themselves in a more roundabout way by taking too many drugs or drinking large amounts of alcohol. Some kids even make "suicide pacts" and die with a friend, boyfriend, or girlfriend.

It may be that by talking about suicide, your friend is simply asking for help. But you can't take the chance she isn't serious. Tell a parent or other adult *immediately* about your concerns for your friend. That adult will be able to get your friend the help she needs.

Q. *My aunt gets really depressed in the winter. Her doctor told her she may have something called seasonal affective disorder. Can kids get that too?*

A. You bet. An estimated **one million American children and teens suffer from winter blues,** also known as seasonal affective disorder (SAD). And once puberty kicks in, four times as many girls as boys get this condition. (Not fair, is it?)

How do you know if you have SAD? You may have it if you become moody or irritable and have trouble concentrating, solely during the fall and winter months.

Researchers don't know for sure what causes these winter blues. Some people may simply be more susceptible to the chemical changes that take place in the brain during the shorter, darker days of winter. When deprived of sunlight, the brain produces more of a hormone called melatonin, which causes sleepiness and sluggishness. In addition, the brain produces less of a hormone called **serotonin,** and serotonin is responsible for regulating moods and producing feelings of well-being.

If you think you suffer from SAD, the main cure is to expose yourself to more light, both natural and artificial. Here are some ways to do this:

❄ **Ask your mom and dad to add a few lamps to the rooms you spend a lot of time in.** Also replace low-wattage bulbs with brighter ones in any existing light fixtures and lamps. Experts believe that exposing  yourself to a minimum of a half hour of extra light a day can greatly improve the symptoms of SAD. You don't have to stare at the lamp, but do make sure that you are facing it, because light enters the body through the eyes.

❄ **Put a timer on your bedside lamp** (available at hardware stores) so it turns on a half hour before you get up. This tricks your brain into thinking there is an extra half hour of daylight. The light will still penetrate your eyelids even if they are closed.

❋ **Get outside.** Even if the sky is gray, the sun's rays still filter through the clouds, and you will gain the benefits of some extra natural light. If stuck inside, sit close to the window, because the sunlight will penetrate the glass.

❋ **Exercise.** Walk or jog around the neighborhood.

(For fun, bring along your dog— who knows, maybe even Fido gets sad in the winter!)

Not only will you get a dose of sunlight, but exercise itself is a proven mood lifter!

Q. *I used to feel pretty confident about myself. But suddenly I feel so insecure. What's going on?*

A. Unfortunately, this is very common among adolescent girls. A nationwide poll commissioned by the American Association of University Women showed that girls ages eight and nine are confident, assertive, and feel good about themselves. In fact, ***60 percent of elementary school girls claimed to be "happy the way I am."*** However, the study showed that when girls reach adolescence, their self-esteem takes a nose dive. By high school, only 29 percent of girls agree with the statement "I'm happy the way I am."

Boys also experience a loss of self-esteem as they enter and navigate the teen years but not as much. In elementary school, 67 percent of boys say they are happy with themselves. By the end of high school, 46 percent still agree with this statement.

What can you do about your LACK of confidence?

Several things:

✳ **Get involved in a sport.** Studies have shown that girls who participate in sports have higher self-esteem. They also tend to do better in school and avoid getting caught up in risky behavior like drinking and doing drugs.

✳ **Stay true to yourself.** If you like to sew, don't blow off the hobby as soon as you hit middle school. Instead, start a sewing club. Girls with strong interests and passions are more confident.

✳ **Stick with math and science.** The study cited above showed that students who like math and science possess significantly greater self-esteem. Unfortunately, as girls grow up, they too often think they are "no good" at these subjects and quit trying. This can cut down their confidence and limit their future career options. If you do find math or science difficult, instead of avoiding the classes, ask your mom and dad if you can have a tutor.

✳ **Spend time with your family.** Research shows that girls who have close family ties and make family a priority feel better about themselves. So sometimes instead of going to a party on Saturday night, hang out with your mom and dad for a wild night of Scrabble®.

Q. *My little sister is four years younger than I am. She is driving me crazy because she always wants to do what I do. For example, if I have a friend over, she wants to hang out with us. What should I do?*

A. While little sisters can be trying, look at things from your
sis's point of view. The reason
she wants to be around you
so much is because she
looks up to you. You are
the revered older sister.
She probably cherishes
every minute she
spends with you.

Therefore, why don't you spend some special time with
her? Bake cookies, do her nails, or fix her doll's hair. Once
she feels she is getting "big sister" attention on a regular
basis, she won't be as needy during times when you want
to be alone or with your friends.

Q. *I used to get along great with my mom and dad. Now suddenly we're fighting all the time about everything: my friends,
school, or the kind of clothes I should wear. What's going on?*

A. It's tough, isn't it? One day you and your parents are talking the same language, the next it feels like you're speak-
ing French and they're answering in Swahili. All you do is
misinterpret each other!

As tough as the misunderstandings and battles may
be, they are completely normal. You and your parents are
beginning the slow process of creating some space
between you. When you were a young child, your parents
were the most important people in your life. You wanted
to spend all your time with them and probably thought
they were darn near perfect.

Now that you're older, their halos are tarnishing a bit. You are able to see them as human after all, with faults just like everyone else. This can be disappointing. At the same time, friends are becoming more important to you.

From your parents' point of view, you're growing up—fast—and they have mixed feelings about that. They see you moving into the world of boys, dating, and makeup, and *they miss the little girl you used to be.* They're also scared that something bad might happen to you, so they start worrying. This concern makes them hold on harder to you—just when you want to be more independent.

The solution is to keep on talking with them. Let them know how you're feeling, and ask them how they're feeling. Don't forget to tell them you love them—and give them chances to tell you they love you, even if it means enduring their childhood terms of endearment, such as Pumpkin Head or Snuggles. With time, as you and your parents adjust to the changes, tensions will lessen.

Q. *My parents are really strict—much more so than other kids' parents. How can I get them to give me more freedom?*

A. First of all, it may help to know that the reason your parents are strict is because they love you and want the best for you.

They care enough to
MAKE RULES
and to spend the time and effort to
ENFORCE THEM.

While you may envy girls who can stay out to all hours of the night, skip homework, or watch MTV until their eyeballs spin in their sockets, in reality, those girls may feel like their parents don't care about them. And sadly, some parents don't as much as they should.

That said, of course it's annoying when other girls can stay out until 10 P.M. and you have to be home by 9 P.M. But there are ways you can get your parents to retool their rules:

✗ *Think of two or three reasons why you should have your privileges extended* and present them in a calm, logical manner. If, for example, you want to break your curfew for a party, your "case" might run like this: **(1)** the event is a one-time occasion that deserves special treatment; **(2)** the party will be chaperoned and no alcohol will be served, so your parents won't have to worry; **(3)** the next day is Sunday and you can sleep in so you won't be missing out on your beauty rest. **(By the way, skip the argument that "everyone is doing it," because your parents are sure to shoot back with a list of those who aren't.)**

If you present your request reasonably (as opposed to whining or complaining), your parents are much more likely to think you are mature enough to handle the new privilege.

✗ *Suggest a compromise.* For example, ask if you can stay out a half hour later, till 9:30, instead of 10. A gradual approach may be easier for your parents to stomach.

✗ *Comply with the rules.* Make sure you are home by 9:30 on the dot. Only by proving to your parents that you are responsible will they feel comfortable giving you more freedom.

Q. *Help! My parents are getting a divorce. My whole world is falling apart. What should I do?*

A. Divorce is one of the roughest things any child can go through. For this reason, you need to talk to both of your parents about your feelings to gain their support and to still feel close to them. It's also a good idea to get some professional help and talk to either a counselor, psychologist, or minister who can help you sort our your feelings.

HANG IN THERE! It's going to be rough for a while, but you will feel better.

Q. *My parents divorced a few years ago, and now my mom has a new boyfriend. I think she's serious about him. It makes me sick. While he's really nice, I just don't want her to marry anyone. What can I do?*

A. You are going through some powerful emotions, all of which are normal. It's hard to see your mom and dad, who you love so much, split up. Then it's even harder to have to open up your life and your heart to a new person in your mom's life.

You also may be worried that if your mom remarries, she won't be as close to you. So you view her boyfriend as competition.

First, talk to your mother. You'll feel better getting your feelings off your chest, and this will give you two a chance to bond and talk honestly about the changes your family may be making. Also, give yourself some time to adjust. As the weeks and months unfold, and you grow more used to the idea of your mom remarrying, the idea will seem more acceptable.

Learn MORE!

What kind of a daughter are you? Sure, you get mad at your parents sometimes and feel like they don't respect you. But do you respect them? Ask yourself, do you answer them when they talk to you? Do you stop and ask about your mom or dad's day? Do you tell them you love them? Maybe with a little extra effort on your part, you'll find you can help smooth over any rough patches with the parental units.

Also ask yourself, what kind of a friend are you? Do you ever

❀ Talk about a pal behind her back?

❀ Fail to stick up for her when others are talking about her?

❀ Focus too much on what you want to do, not what she wants to do?

❀ Take her for granted by maybe asking her to do a lot of favors for you or by not appreciating her friendship?

Think about your answers and how you can become an even better friend and daughter. After all, family and friends are important—and it's always a good idea to work on being the best person you can.

$\mathcal{F}$ood for Thought: Nutrition and Eating Disorders

$\mathcal{A}$s a kid, I was a junk food junkie. Ding Dongs®, Oreos®, Milk Duds®, Lucky Charms® cereal (just the marshmallow candies, forget the actual cereal)—I loved them all. One of my favorite after-school snacks was a Fudgsicle®, chocolate chips, and pretzels, all eaten together.

Ironically, my mother and sister were always on diets. They were such healthful eaters, always nibbling on salads and broiled chicken breasts.

Because I was pretty thin, I didn't think much about nutrition. Hey, as long as I wasn't fat, who cared what I ate? But then in junior high, I started to feel really tired in the afternoons. I couldn't concentrate in class. One day I was talking to my mom about the problem, and she asked, "What are you eating for lunch in the cafeteria?" I thought about it and replied, "I usually buy two chocolate chip cookies." (And let me tell you, they were the best thing in the cafeteria: soft, chewy, and loaded with chocolate chips.)

My mom took one look at me and said, "If you don't eat better at lunch, you'll always feel sick. You need to start eating a sandwich and some fruit."

As much as it pained me to listen to Mom, I did. And guess what? After a few days of eating sandwiches, I perked up and quit feeling so tired and lethargic after lunch.

Q. *I hear a lot about the four food groups. What are they?*

A. The four food groups are

1 **DAIRY PRODUCTS,** such as cheese, cottage cheese, yogurt, and milk. These are *good sources of calcium,* which helps strengthen bones and teeth.

2 **FRUITS AND VEGETABLES.** These are a *good source of vitamin C,* especially oranges, grapefruit, and tomatoes. Vitamin C is important in maintaining the connective tissue in our bodies and helping to heal wounds.

Fruits and vegetables also contain potassium, which helps the kidneys as well as the heart and other muscles function properly. Also, the fiber in fruits and veggies helps you digest food.

3 **GRAINS,** such as cereals, bread, rice, and pasta. These foods are a major source of complex carbohydrates, which *supply readily available energy to the body* in the form of blood sugar.

They also contain essential vitamins and fiber. In addition, whole grains supply iron, which is very important for growing girls.

4 **MEAT OR MEAT SUBSTITUTES,** such as poultry, fish, shellfish, eggs, nuts, peanut butter, legumes (peas and beans), and tofu. These foods are rich in protein. *Protein is needed to help build up your cells and body tissues.* It also helps your body digest food and form hormones, among other important functions.

Q. *I admit it. I'm not the healthiest eater. I don't always like to eat fruits and vegetables. So tell me, how much should I be eating of each food group every day?*

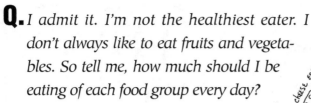

A. Here's what you should be shooting for:

✔ **Three servings** of milk, yogurt, or cheese. One serving equals a cup of low-fat milk or yogurt or 1½ to 2 ounces of cheese.

✔ **Two to four servings** of fruit. One medium piece of fruit, ¾ cup of fruit juice, or ½ cup of canned fruit equals one serving.

✔ **Three to five servings** of vegetables. One serving equals ½ cup of raw or cooked veggies or 1 cup of leafy raw vegetables.

✔ **Two to three servings** of meat, poultry, fish, beans, eggs, or nuts. One serving equals 2½ to 3 ounces of cooked lean meat, poultry, or fish, or ½ cup cooked beans.

✔ **Six to eleven servings** of bread, cereal, rice, or pasta. One serving equals one slice of bread; ½ cup of cooked pasta, rice, or cereal, or 1 ounce of ready-to-eat cereal.

Fats, oils, and sweets should be ***eaten sparingly***.

Q. *I am a cookie-aholic. I also love to nosh on chips. But I'm worried about what I'm doing to my body. Should I stop eating these foods?*

A. You're smart to be concerned about the kinds of food you are consuming. Now that your body is growing and developing at a dramatic rate, it's more important than ever that you eat right.

By the way, it's also important that you eat enough. The average 11- to 14-year-old girl requires 2,400 calories a day; the average 15- to18-year-old needs 2,100.

> **FASCINATING FACTOID**
>
> Just as you always suspected, guys can eat more than girls. The average 15- to 18-year-old boy needs around 3,000 calories a day; girls 15 to 18 require just 2,100.

Studies are showing that the better you eat now, the less likely you are to run into such health problems as heart disease when you are adult.

The good news is, you don't have to give up eating chips and cookies altogether. All you have to do is **eat them in moderation.** For example, instead of eating ten cookies, stick to two or three. Limit yourself to two handfuls of chips instead of half the bag. You'll feel better and be doing your body a big favor.

Q. *My mom is always telling me I need to eat protein. Why?*

A. Protein helps your cells to grow and repair themselves. Most nutritionists recommend that during puberty, **girls eat about 80 grams of protein daily.** That's about 15 percent of the total calories you eat.

You can get protein by eating beef, poultry, and fish.

However, if you don't eat much meat, there are still many other ways you can add protein to your diet. Milk and milk products (such as cheese), eggs, tofu, nuts, and beans are all good sources of protein.

Q. *My best friend is a carrot fiend. She nibbles on them all the time. When I ask her why, she says, "Because they are low in calories and high in fiber." What is fiber?*

A. Fiber is the part of fruits, vegetables, whole grains, and bran that passes through the body without being digested. As it is carried through the digestive system, fiber helps to keep your digestive system working well, lowers the level of **cholesterol** in the blood, and may even lower the risk of some diseases, such as cancer.

Each of us needs about 20 to 30 grams of fiber a day— a little less than an ounce. Some foods that are rich in fiber include

▲ **Breads and cereals:** bran flakes, raisin bran, bran muffin, oatmeal, popcorn, brown rice.

▲ **Fruits:** apple, pear, strawberries, prunes.

▲ **Vegetables:** broccoli, corn, potato with skin, carrots.

▲ **Legumes:** peas, kidney beans, lima beans, lentils.

▲ **Nuts:** peanuts, almonds.

Q. *I snack all day long instead of eating big meals because I get full so quickly. Is that OK?*

A. Yes, as long as you are eating healthy snacks. In fact, many nutritionists believe it is better for your body to eat five or six small meals throughout the day rather than three big meals. Among some healthy snacks to reach for when you are on the run are these:

◆ Fresh and dried fruits.

◆ Raw veggies.

◆ Whole-grain crackers.

◆ Yogurt.

◆ Bagel.

◆ Milk (nonfat or 1 percent).

Avoid foods that are high in fat and sugar, such as candy, cake, potato chips, cookies, and soft drinks.

Q. *I'm not hungry in the morning. How important is it to eat breakfast?*

A. You are not alone—**50 percent of teens don't eat breakfast.** However, if you don't eat anything in the morning, you run the risk of becoming tired and possibly having trouble concentrating at school. The nutrients gained from breakfast will help you to think more clearly and efficiently.

However, you are also doing your body a disservice if you load up on sweetened cereals or sugary, high-fat foods like doughnuts first thing in the morning. These foods offer little nutritional value. Plus, while they may give you an energy boost, a half hour later all that sugar will make you feel more tired and lethargic than ever.

Instead of skipping breakfast or eating sugary foods in the morning, start out the day right by trying some of these foods:

- Bagel with cream cheese.
- Bowl of oatmeal.
- Raisin bran or bran flakes with bananas or strawberries.
- Piece of wheat toast with peanut butter.

Try eating breakfast for a day or two, and see how you feel. Chances are, you'll feel more energetic than usual and be hooked on the breakfast routine.

Q. *My mother has started cooking without salt and putting the entire family on a low-sodium diet. Why is eating salt so bad for you?*

A. People who eat too much salt put themselves at risk for high blood pressure and other health problems. They also may retain water and become bloated, and who needs that?

Think about this: 1 teaspoon of salt contains 2,800 milligrams of sodium. But your body needs only a fraction of that amount to meet its daily sodium requirements. Kudos to your mom, who is making sure your family stays healthy.

However, when Mom's not around, here's **what YOU can do to cut down on your sodium intake:**

* Don't salt foods.
* Avoid processed meats, which contain high sodium levels.
* Replace salt with lemon juice for extra zest.
* Add little or no salt in cooking water for pasta, rice, and cereals.
* Cut down on high-sodium condiments, such as soy sauce and ketchup.

NOT ALL FATS ARE CREATED EQUAL

There are three kinds of fats: saturated, polyunsaturated, and monounsaturated. Saturated fat is thought to be the type that leads to health problems. On the other hand, polyunsaturated and monounsaturated fats may help lower blood cholesterol levels, which is good for your health. (But keep in mind that all fats are high in calories and, again, should be eaten in moderation.)

Saturated Fats
Butter • Cheese • Chocolate • Coconut and coconut oil
Egg yolk • Meat • Milk • Poultry

Polyunsaturated Fats
Corn oil • Cottonseed oil • Tuna and salmon
Safflower oil • Sesame seed oil

Monounsaturated Fats
Cashews • Olives and olive oil • Peanuts and peanut oil
Almonds • Peanut butter • Avocados

✳ Choose unsalted pretzels and chips over their salty counterparts (at first these may seem bland, but you will soon get used to the taste).

✳ Opt for packaged food or soups labeled "low in sodium."

Q. *I know I am supposed to avoid foods that have a lot of fat. But is it really that bad to eat fat?*

A. Fats have a rotten reputation for a good reason. A diet high in fat may lead to heart disease and cancer. Also, fats contain more than twice the calories per unit weight as do carbohydrates or protein. This means that ounce for ounce, they can cause more unwanted weight gain than other foods. Most

nutritionists therefore recommend that only about 30 percent of your total daily calories should come from fats.

**On the other hand, eating TOO FEW
fats can be bad for your health.** Fats fulfill
many important roles in your body. They cushion your
bones and organs, aid in building cells, and help transport
needed vitamins throughout your body, among other
things. The key to maintaining good health isn't to give up
fats, but to eat them **IN MODERATION.**

What foods have a high fat content?

✖ Fried foods (french fries, fried chicken, doughnuts).

✖ Rich foods (pastries, ice cream, heavy sauces).

✖ Greasy foods (bacon).

✖ Toppings (butter, mayonnaise, margarine).

✖ Muffins.

✖ Some crackers.

Q. *I love fast food. But is it terrible for me?*

A. As long as you aren't eating it morning, noon, and night,
it's OK to occasionally eat some fast food at your favorite
drive-through. The problem with eating too much fast food
is that foods such as burgers and fries tend to be high in
fat, calories, and sodium.

However, fast-food restaurants are becoming more
nutrition aware, and it's possible to eat relatively well at
some of them. They may offer, for example, salads, fat-free
muffins, low-fat milks and yogurts, and grilled foods
instead of fried ones. Scan the menus carefully the next
time you go to your neighborhood drive-through and see

ORDER UP GOOD NUTRITION

Want to eat better even at your favorite fast-food restaurant? Here's how:

☆ Avoid mayonnaise and salad dressing, which are loaded with fat.

☆ Choose grilled or broiled foods rather than fried ones.

☆ Order plain burgers or cheeseburgers instead of ones with secret (and usually fatty) sauces.

☆ Cut down on ketchup, mustard, and pickles to decrease sodium intake.

☆ If ordering pizza, choose a vegetable topping and a thin crust. Avoid processed meats like bacon, pepperoni, and sausage, which are high in fat and sodium.

☆ Drink milk instead of sodas.

☆ Order a baked potato instead of fries.

☆ Remove the skin from fried chicken.

what healthy foods are available. Instead of ordering fries with your burger, try opting for a green salad—just watch it on the salad dressing.

Q. *I hear a lot about good carbohydrates versus bad carbohydrates. What is the difference?*

A. Carbohydrates give your body the energy it needs to keep going each day. There are two types: simple and complex. **Simple carbohydrates are mostly SUGAR—** high in calories with little nutritional benefit. They give you an energy boost because your body absorbs them quickly, but soon afterward you feel tired again. Candy, sodas, sugary breakfast cereals, doughnuts, and fruit juices are loaded with simple carbs.

Complex carbohydrates, on the other hand, are gradually absorbed into the bloodstream and provide longlasting ENERGY. These are found in whole-wheat breads, cereals, beans, pasta, and fruits and veggies. These complex carbs should make up 50 to 60 percent of your diet each day.

It's OK to nibble once in a while on simple carb foods, but to keep your body growing and running smoothly, load up on the complex carbs.

Q. *How important is it that I eat a lot of calcium? I know milk contains it, but I don't like milk!*

A. It's very important that you consume enough calcium. During puberty, your body needs more calcium than during any other time in your life. Your developing bones need the added calcium to grow into their full potential and to ensure that the amount of new bone you produce now is enough to last you a lifetime.

As women grow older, they're prone to osteoporosis, a loss of bone volume. You can help prevent this disease now by getting your bones off to a healthy start.

Even if you don't drink milk, you can still get the daily calcium you need by eating milk products, such as cheese and yogurt. Other foods rich in calcium include broccoli, greens (such as spinach and kale), and almonds.

However, if it's not only milk you don't like but all dairy products, you may need calcium supplements. Ask your doctor for more information.

Q. *How much iron do I need to eat every day? And please don't tell me the only way I can get it is through eating spinach. Yuck!*

A. Don't worry. **POPEYE may have gotten his strength through SPINACH, but there are many other sources of iron out there.**

Yes, you do need iron. The American Academy of Pediatrics recommends that girls (and boys) consume 18 milligrams of iron daily. Your body needs this iron so its enzymes can function properly and so it can replenish the iron lost during your period. You also can lose iron when you work up a big sweat exercising.

If you aren't getting enough iron in your diet, you may suffer from a disease called **iron-deficiency anemia,** which is a lack of iron in the body. Anemia can make you tired and listless.

You can become an iron woman by eating the following foods:

❑ Strawberries.

❑ Apple, prune, or tomato juice.

❑ Broccoli.

❑ Green peas.

❑ Sweet potatoes.

❑ Spinach *(sorry!)*.

❑ Bran flakes with raisins.

❑ Pork, beef, or veal.

❑ Navy, lima, or lentil beans.

To enhance the absorption of iron, eat foods containing generous amounts of vitamin C (such as citrus fruits and green vegetables) in combination with high-iron foods.

If you suspect that you may have an iron deficiency (you are feeling tired or listless), see your doctor.

Q. *A friend of mine is always popping vitamins. I don't, and she says I'm crazy. Do I need to be taking vitamin supplements to stay healthy?*

A. Probably not, as long as you are eating a healthy, well-balanced diet from the four food groups. **A good diet should supply all the vitamins you need.**

In fact, taking too many vitamins can actually be harmful. Excessive vitamin A can cause peeling of the skin, increased pressure on the brain, changes in bone, and hair loss. Too much vitamin D can lead to a calcium buildup in the blood, which can in turn lead to kidney stones. Taking too much vitamin C can also lead to kidney stones. Excessive vitamin E can interfere with the metabolism of other vitamins, causing bleeding problems or an upset stomach.

Q. *Can you explain what certain vitamins do and how you can get them in your diet?*

A. Here's the rundown on the essential vitamins your body needs:

❋ **Vitamin A helps your vision and immune system, among other important functions.** You can find it in whole milk, apricots, carrots, squash, butter, liver, and some green leafy veggies.

❀ **Vitamin C strengthens your bones and blood vessels and helps your body's wounds heal.** You can find it in citrus fruits, strawberries, lettuce, broccoli, tomatoes, and green leafy vegetables.

❀ **Vitamin D helps keep your bones strong and healthy.** You can find it in milk, canned fish, eggs, and butter (as well as sunlight).

❀ **Vitamin E helps your lungs and immune system function.** You can find it in vegetable oils, peanut oils, almonds, hazelnuts, whole-wheat flour, spinach, lettuce, and onion.

❀ **Vitamin B_6 aids in the formation of red blood cells.** You can find it in fish, meat, poultry, whole grains, fruits, and green vegetables.

❀ **Vitamin B_{12} helps your nervous system function properly.** You can find it in animal products, such as meat, fish, eggs, and milk.

❀ **Thiamine, niacin, and riboflavin all help your body produce energy from nutrients.** You can find these B vitamins in meats, fish, whole-grain breads, cereals, and nuts.

❀ **Folic acid, another B vitamin, helps produce red blood cells.** You can find it in liver, beans, citrus, poultry, shellfish, and leafy green vegetables.

Q. *I know I'm supposed to avoid foods with high cholesterol. But why?*

A. Cholesterol is a waxy, fatty substance found only in animal products such as meat, egg yolks, and cheese. There is good evidence that eating too much of it can ultimately lead to heart disease and heart attacks.

Q. *If I don't drink coffee, can I still be consuming a lot of caffeine?*

A. You sure can. Tea, soft drinks, and chocolate are loaded with caffeine. It's best to avoid caffeine, because it can cause many bad side effects, such as anxiety, irritability, headaches, and sleeplessness. So the next time you reach for that diet soda, grab a glass of water instead.

Q. *A lot of my friends walk around all day with a bottle of water. Are they just being cool, or is it really good for you to drink a lot of water?*

A. Water is definitely in— there are even bars now where all you can order are different kinds of water—and for a good reason. Water performs many important functions in the body:

FASCINATING **F**ACTOID

When you break down almost any food you eat, 85 to 96 percent of it is water.

✳ It helps the body regulate its temperature.

✳ It aids the body in digestion, absorption, circulation, and elimination.

✳ It washes food through the digestive system.

✳ It shuttles oxygen and nutrients to the cells.

For all of these reasons, doctors recommend that we all **drink six to eight 8-ounce glasses of water a day**—and more in hot weather. And don't wait until you're thirsty to drink up—if you are thirsty, it means your body is already getting dehydrated. If you

Cool fact Water makes up 60 percent of our body weight.

are even slightly dehydrated, you may have trouble concentrating and get irritated easily.

Q. *I love the food labels on the backs of products because it's easy to see what exactly is in something I'm eating. But I'm confused about some of the terms. For example, what does it really mean if a food is labeled "low-fat" or "light"?*

A. The labels providing breakdowns of nutrients allow all of us to become smarter consumers. However, as you've noticed, it's hard to always know what the terms on some product labels mean. Here's a rundown of some of the most common labels you'll find:

★ **"Low-cholesterol."** This means an individual food can contain no more than 20 milligrams of cholesterol per typical serving (and saturated fat can't exceed two grams, because it raises blood cholesterol). On a meal or main dish, "low cholesterol" means no more than 20 milligrams per 100 grams of food. This translates to about 60 milligrams in a 10-ounce dish or meal.

★ **"Low-fat."** For individual foods, a food can contain no more than 3 grams of fat per typical serving. "Low fat" on a meal or main dish essentially means no more than 30 percent of its calories can come from fat. The Center for Science in the Public Interest recommends looking for no more than 2 grams of fat per 100 calories (20 percent).

★ **"Low in saturated fat."** Individual foods can have no more than 1 gram of saturated fat per serving. A meal or main dish can usually make this claim if less than 10 percent of its calories come from saturated fat.

★ **"Low sodium."** An individual food can contain 140 milligrams or less per serving. For main dishes or meals, this means 140 milligrams or less per 100 grams. This translates to 400 milligrams of sodium in a typical 10-ounce meal or entree—which is low.

★ **"Light" or "lite."** This means different things. If the food starts out fatty, "light" means that at least half of its fat has been removed. This applies to cheese, hot dogs, and other foods that initially get half or more of their calories from fat.

Less-fatty foods are "light" if *either* the fat content has been cut in half or the calories have been cut by a third. The label will tell you which.

A main dish or meal is "light" if it meets the definition of *either* low-calorie or low-fat. "Light" may refer to color or texture, but the label must tell you so. "Light" can also mean half the usual sodium content or less, but the label must read "light in sodium."

★ **"Lean."** This means less than 10 grams of fat, less than 4 grams of saturated fat, and less than 95 milligrams of cholesterol.

LABEL, LABEL, ON THE BOX, WHICH IS THE HEALTHIEST FOOD OF ALL?

What is in a label? To help consumers, the Center for Science in the Public Interest breaks down some of the most important parts of a typical label you'll find on the back of packaged food. Here's what you are really reading:

"Serving Size": Make sure to check this because if you eat more or less of what's listed, you will have to adjust the other numbers accordingly.

"Calories from fat": This helps you see how fatty a food is. Watch out if this number is more than a third of the calories.

"Daily Value": This tells you how much of a day's worth of fat, sodium, etc., the food provides. The Center's recommendation: If a food has 20 percent or more of the DV, it's "high" in the nutrient. "Low" means no more than 5 percent.

"Sugars": There is no percentage listed under the "Daily Value" because health authorities have not set a limit on how much sugar we should eat each day. The Center recommends 50 grams or less a day.

"Percent Daily Values are based . . .": This will be the same on all labels.

★ **"Extra lean."** This means less than 5 grams of fat, less than 2 grams of saturated fat, and less than 95 milligrams of cholesterol.

Source: *Center for Science in the Public Interest*

Q. *I am 30 pounds overweight. I need to start a diet but don't know how.*

A. Give yourself a pat on the back. It's great that you want to start becoming more healthy.

Obesity is a real problem in this country. SOME 10 PERCENT OF PREADOLESCENTS AND 15 PERCENT OF ADOLESCENTS ARE OBESE. And that number is rising: There has been almost a 40 percent increase in obesity among adolescents in the past 15 years, partly due to teens' high-fat diets and lack of vigorous exercise.

What does it mean to be obese anyway? Most doctors use the term *obese* when a person's weight is more than 20 percent above what researchers have determined is desirable for that person's age, height, and sex.

Obesity is caused by many factors, some of which may be out of your control, such as heredity. Some people are born with a slower metabolism—the rate at which a body breaks down calories—which can cause weight gain. This explains why some girls gain weight eating just two cookies while others can finish off an entire box and never gain an ounce.

Obesity comes with many problems. Overweight people often feel alone and unaccepted. Physically, obesity takes its toll on a body and may ultimately cause high blood pressure, diabetes, stroke, muscle aches, and back pain.

To lose weight, visit your family doctor. He or she should be able to recommend a sensible weight loss plan as well as put you in touch with a nutritionist. Together, you can come up with a safe, sensible eating plan.

Your family doctor and a nutritionist also can steer you clear of any fad diets or diets that are too restrictive and cause you to lose too much too quickly—putting you at risk for just as quickly putting the weight back on. The best diets are those that promote a slow, safe weight loss.

Q. *I keep hearing about girls at school who have an eating disorder. How common are such disorders?*

A. Unfortunately, eating disorders are all too common. Conservative estimates indicate that 5 to 10 percent of women and girls—that's 5 to 10 million women and girls in the United States—suffer from an eating disorder. Put another way, this means that **in a school of 1,000 kids, 50 to 100 are struggling with an eating disorder.**

Most girls who develop an eating disorder start out innocently enough. They just want to drop a few pounds, but then quickly lose control of their behavior. Instead of feeling thin, beautiful, and popular as they had hoped, they suffer from fatigue, shame, and self-disgust. They often feel trapped in a prison of calories and food—a prison they worry they created and feel they can never escape from.

There are three types of eating disorders:

Anorexia nervosa. This is when a girl extremely restricts her food intake and experiences excessive weight loss. People with anorexia have a distorted body image. Even though a girl may be very thin, when she looks in the mirror she "sees" a fat person. Girls who participate in sports such as ballet, ice-skating, and gymnastics are statistically more likely to engage in self-starvation due to the pressures these sports put on them to be thin.

Bulimia nervosa. This is a cycle of binge eating followed by purging through vomiting, laxative use, or overexercise. Binging is when a girl eats more in a short period of time than the average person would. Binge eating often includes a feeling of lack of control over what is eaten, how much is eaten, and how to stop eating. Sometimes girls are both anorexic and bulimic.

Despite what you may think, bulimics are often of average weight or overweight. Purging does not rid the body of all the food ingested during a binge.

Binge-eating disorder. Compulsive overeating is characterized by repeated episodes of overeating or eating more than the average person would in a short period of time. Eating is often an attempt to fill an emotional void or to cover up or avoid painful feelings.

All of these eating disorders are very dangerous. Eating Disorders Awareness and Prevention (EDAP) estimates that over your lifetime, 50,000 individuals will die as a result of complications from their eating disorders.

Q. *What are the risks of having an eating disorder?*

A. People with eating disorders put a huge strain on their bodies that can ultimately kill them. Let's look at some of the physical and emotional dangers a girl with an eating disorder exposes herself to.

Self-starvation can lead to dehydration, malnutrition, and electrolyte imbalance. These can cause low blood pressure, heart problems, and even death. Other physical symptoms include pale, dry skin; **`thinning hair`**; and light-headedness. Emotionally, girls with anorexia may suffer from depression, suicidal tendencies, feelings of worthlessness, and chronic fatigue.

Bulimics can suffer from low blood pressure and a high heart rate. Abuse of laxatives and diuretics can cause digestive problems and **`severe dehydration`**. Vomiting can cause a girl's face and the whites of her eyes to fill with broken blood vessels. **`Her teeth may decay`** from having frequent contact with the acidic contents of the stomach. And the esophagus, the tube leading from the mouth to the stomach, can become inflamed or torn. Emotionally, bulimics may suffer from **`depression and mood swings`**.

Binge eaters put themselves at risk for obesity. They may also suffer from high blood pressure and high cholesterol. Compulsive eaters tend to be overcome with feelings of depression, shame, and guilt.

Q. *How do you know if a person has an eating disorder?*

A. Here are some warning signs to look for:

WARNING SIGNS OF ANOREXIA NERVOSA

- intense fear of gaining weight or becoming fat even when underweight
- inner value or happiness determined by weight or size
- refusal to eat certain foods
- sudden and/or drastic weight loss
- cooks for others but refuses to eat what is cooked
- talks or thinks about food, weight, calories, or dieting all the time

● desperate to exercise to burn off calories even when sick, injured, or in bad weather

WARNING SIGNS OF BULIMIA

● frequent trips to the bathroom

● collecting and stashing food

● eating large amounts of food in one sitting

● extreme eating habits (strict diet-ing, then overeating)

● desperate to exercise to burn off calories when sick, injured, or in bad weather

WARNINGS SIGNS OF COMPULSIVE OVEREATING

● collecting and stashing food

● eating large amounts of food in one sitting

● extreme eating habits (strict dieting, then overeating)

Q. *What causes someone to have an eating disorder?*

A. Experts believe that a variety of factors, pressures, and expectations can lead to an eating disorder.

▶ *The perfectionist trap.* Girls with anorexia or bulimia are often perfectionists. They may feel pressure to be "perfect" or to look like an ultraskinny fashion model. They may also see restricting food as a way to gain control over their life when they feel it's out of control.

▶ *Parental problems.* Physical, emotional, or sexual abuse or neglect can contribute to the development of an eating disorder. High expectations and pressures held by parents or family members can also contribute to the problem.

▶ *The "thin is in" culture.* Generally, the media and American culture place a high value on being thin and physically attractive. A girl's peers reinforce the culture's standard of beauty (which is usually impossible to meet), and a girl may feel pressured to starve herself to attain this unattainable standard.

▶ *Other emotional problems.* Eating disorders may be a girl's way of avoiding, expressing, or relieving painful feelings such as anger or fear.

Q. *Do boys get anorexia?*

A. Anorexia and bulimia is not just a "girl" disease. **At least one million boys and men are struggling with an eating disorder.** Boys in sports such as wrestling, where they must maintain a certain body weight to compete, are especially at risk.

Q. *Over the last year I have lost 25 pounds. Everyone says I look really thin, but to me, I'm still fat. Some days all I eat are pretzels. I'm worried I may have anorexia. What should I do?*

A. Please get help immediately. If you feel comfortable doing so, begin by telling your parents. They can arrange for you to see a doctor and start getting you the help you need. If you don't feel comfortable talking to your parents, get help from another adult you trust, such as the school counselor or an aunt. Or you can call the National Association of Anorexia Nervosa and Associated Disorders at (847) 831-3438 to receive a referral to a local eating disorder therapist. You can also call EDAP at (800) 931-2237.

Eating disorders are devastating to go through, but

with professional help, you can overcome yours. Once you get your problem out in the open, you can obtain the treatment you need. Many hospitals now offer comprehensive treatment programs where you can get both medical attention and psychological counseling. **DON'T WAIT ANOTHER DAY. GET HELP RIGHT NOW.**

Q. *I have a friend who is constantly worried about her weight even though she is thin. I don't think she's anorexic or bulimic, but can you still have a problem with food even if you aren't?*

A. Yes, you can. In fact, there is a term for this problem, and it's called disordered eating. While disordered eating is not as severe as an eating disorder, it is still very troubling and can lead to an eating disorder. Some experts in the field believe that over half of all girls suffer or at some point will suffer from disordered eating.

What are some symptoms of disordered eating?

○ Restricting calories or not eating certain foods because they are "fattening."

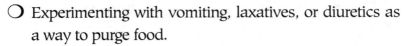

○ Thinking about food constantly.

○ Having a negative body image.

○ Having an irrational fear of getting fat.

○ Experimenting with vomiting, laxatives, or diuretics as a way to purge food.

○ Getting hooked on diet pills.

Having disordered eating comes with a host of potentially dangerous physical and emotional problems. For starters, it can lead to a full-blown eating disorder. Also, experimenting with laxatives, diuretics, and diet pills can have all sorts of bad effects on your body. Not eating enough can make you tired, cause you to lose your period, and damage your hair and skin.

Many girls with eating disorders are depressed. Some isolate themselves from friends or social activities because they don't want to be around food.

You should talk to your friend and tell her you are concerned. Suggest that she talk to a trusted adult who can get her some help. If she refuses, alert an adult to her condition. She needs help now before her disordered eating turns into a potentially life-threatening eating disorder.

Learn MORE!

You may think you are eating a well-balanced diet, but how well are you *really* eating? Find out by writing down everything (yes, every little thing) you eat each day for a week. Don't cheat—halves of cookies and nibbling count! Don't worry about writing down how many calories you consume—you're not trying to lose weight, just eat better!

At the end of a week, check and see if you have been eating judiciously from all four food groups. Are you getting enough veggies and fruit, or are you bread and pasta heavy?

Then write down what changes you could make to have a healthier diet. Try to incorporate these changes into next week's diet. If you can stick to your changes for a week or two, then a month or two, you'll find that healthy eating is becoming a way of life.

CHAPTER 10

Treating Your Body Right: Saying Yes to Exercise and No to Drugs and Alcohol

When I was in sixth grade, my dad got a great idea. "Let's build a volleyball court in the backyard," he said. So we did.

Every night after dinner in the spring and summer, our family would round up all the neighbors for the biggest game of junk volleyball you've ever seen. We hit the volleyball in ways I'm sure no one had ever—or will ever again—hit one. Then my dad bought a badminton set, a really cheap one, and we added that game to our evening lineup. Again, we were terrible.

I figured I was hopeless in both sports until I joined a volleyball team in junior high school. The coach actually taught me some skills, and I started to improve. By the time I got to high school, I was pretty good. So was my sister. Somehow we also got pretty good at badminton. We played varsity volleyball and badminton and even made it to the regional quarter-final badminton championship in doubles our senior year. Some of my happiest moments were spent in my high school gym.

I later went on to play both sports in college, along with soccer. Sports gave me a way to make friends and fit in, as well as a little bit of celebrity status. And I guess I owe it all to my dad.

Q. *I admit it. I'm a couch potato. I see all these other girls out running or biking and becoming total sweat bombs, and I just don't get it. Why is it so important to exercise?*

A. Exercise strengthens your heart, lungs, and circulatory system and helps prevent heart disease. It lowers your blood pressure and cholesterol level. Weight-bearing activities, where you are on your feet, such as walking, jogging, or soccer, help keep your bones strong and healthy. In addition, working out burns fat and calories.

If that's not enough to convince you to get off the couch, get this: Lots of evidence shows that staying fit will help you fight off disease and live longer.

Working out also relieves stress and depression. Research has demonstrated that just going for a brisk walk is one of the best things you can do to beat a blue mood.

And yep, when you exercise, you're going to S W E A T, but try it—you may even like it, perspiration and all!

Q. *I really want to get in shape, but I'm not sure how to start. I've never really participated in a sport before. Do you have any advice?*

A. The first thing to do is talk to your family doctor and get some fitness recommendations from him or her. This is especially important if you've had any medical problems or are taking medications that may make certain activities off-limits.

Next, choose a sport you really enjoy. Also, set small goals when starting out. For example, if you begin swimming, don't expect to log in a mile on your first day or you'll either injure yourself or become discouraged when you can't cover more than a quarter of a mile. Instead, set goals you can realistically achieve and you feel good about. Then readjust them as you gain confidence, endurance, and skills.

Q. *A good friend of mine started running and, within a month or two, injured her knee. Now she can't do anything! How can I make sure I don't get an injury?*

A. There is no foolproof way to make sure you never twist an ankle or get a shin splint. That said, here are a few commonsense rules to follow to protect yourself against injuries:

✳ **Be shoe savvy.** Choose shoes that give your feet enough support or cushioning so your muscles and joints don't take too much of a pounding. Also make sure the shoes fit correctly so you don't develop painful blisters or calluses.

✳ **Stretch it out.** Before hitting the hiking trail or the soccer field, gently warm up your muscles by stretching for 5 minutes. Stretching is part of any good fitness routine. As you stretch, try not to bounce. Hold each stretch for 5 to 10 seconds. If your muscles are cold, you are more likely to pull a muscle. (By the way, stretching has another big benefit: The more limber you are now, the more flexible you'll be your entire life, even when you're a grandma.)

❋ **Know when to stop.** If you feel a sharp pain while working out, stop for the day. If you push an injured body part, the injury will just get worse.

❋ **Cool down.** After you are finished exercising, spend 5 minutes cooling down. For example, if you've gone out for a run, slow down to a fast walk, and then walk slowly for a few minutes. Gradually winding down your activity can go a long way to avoiding injuries.

Q. *I've made the resolution to finally get in shape. How much exercise should I be getting? Please don't tell me I need a few hours each day, because my schedule is packed with school and drama.*

A. You don't need to spend a lot of time to be in shape. Most fitness experts recommend at least 30 minutes of aerobic exercise three to five times a week.

Aerobic exercise is any activity that elevates your heart rate for a sustained amount of time, such as running, biking, dancing, swimming, or hiking. AEROBIC EXERCISE IS GOOD FOR YOU because it trains your heart and lungs to work more efficiently.

Q. *At the Y, I saw a poster that mentioned reaching your target heart rate while exercising. What does this mean?*

Cool fact

Exercise isn't your thing? No sweat. Speed walk around the mall while window-shopping. You can burn between 200 and 500 calories, depending on how fast you go.

A. A **target heart rate** is
the ideal rate your heart
should be beating to get
the full benefit of the
workout. If your heart is
beating too slowly, your
cardiovascular system
isn't being pushed hard
enough.

There is also some-
thing called the maxi-
mum average heart rate.
This is the hardest your heart can work.

To find your target rate (it depends on your age) **subtract your age from 220.** This is your maximum heart rate. **Take 65 to 75 percent of your
maximum heart rate** and you'll have your target
heart rate.

While exercising, it's a good idea to check your heart
rate. To do this:

1 Put your index and middle fingers on your wrist or the
side of your neck and find your pulse.

2 Count the number of times your heart beats during a
10-second period.

3 Multiply that number by 6, and you will have the
number of times your heart is beating per minute.

Q. *I like to run, which is great aerobic exercise and works my legs.
But what about the rest of my body, like my arms and stomach?*

A. You can do exercises such as sit-ups and push-ups to tone and strengthen these muscles. You can also lift weights to increase muscle strength. (But first check with your doctor; not all recommend that preteens use weights). Strength  training, aerobic exercise, and stretching are the three essential components of fitness. Ask your PE teacher for some strengthening moves to try.

Q. *I really want to get in shape but can't get motivated. Can you help?*

A. If you're having trouble catching the fitness bug, here are some tricks that may help you get moving:

✳ *Start small.* Tell yourself, "I'm just going to exercise for 15 minutes. If, at the end of the 15 minutes, I feel like quitting, I will." Most of the time, once you've gone to all the trouble of putting on your workout clothes and shoes, you'll keep going after the 15 minutes are up.

✳ *Buddy up.* Studies show that you are more likely to stick with an exercise routine if you have a partner who is counting on you to work out with him or her. So grab a friend and exercise together.

✳ *Be consistent.* Research also shows that people who work out at the same time each day tend to stick to it more. That's because the workout becomes a habit. When 4 P.M. rolls around, you just know it's time to hit the running path!

✳ *Bribe yourself.* Promise yourself that after you are done with your workout, you'll **GIVE YOURSELF A SMALL REWARD.** Maybe you'll listen to your favorite CD, call a friend, or buy a new magazine. Pairing pleasure with the possible pain of exercise will make you more likely to go for it!

Q. *A lot of girls I know hate to exercise. I have the opposite problem. If I don't exercise every day, I feel terrible about myself! And sometimes I work out so hard, I feel really tired afterward. Is there such a thing as working out too much?*

A. There certainly is. While it's wonderful that you enjoy being fit, you may be overdoing it. Remember, to stay in shape, all you need to do is work out three to five times a week for at least a half hour. Overexercising comes with a number of risks:

✳ You are more likely to get an injury because you are overstraining your body.

✳ You may develop amenorrhea (when periods stop or are skipped), which can lead to fragile bones in adulthood.

✳ You become overfatigued and can't concentrate on school or even fun things like friends.

✳ You may develop something called exercise bulimia, where girls get unhealthfully hooked on exercise as a way to lose weight.

Of course, some serious athletes have to train more than the average girl because the coach and the team demand it. Other girls work out more because a certain sport or activity is their passion in life.

How to know if you are overexercising and may even be at risk for exercise bulimia? **Warning signs to watch for:**

✳ You work out even when you don't feel well or are injured.

✳ You hate yourself or feel guilty if you miss a workout.

✳ Your period stops or you skip some months.

✳ You worry you'll gain weight if you don't exercise, even for only a single day.

If you think your attitude toward exercise is turning unhealthy, talk to your family doctor, a school nurse, or counselor. Exercise addiction often masks emotional upsets such as grief, depression, and low self-esteem—issues needing the help of a professional.

Q. *I know a few kids who have started drinking. They say there are so many worse things they could be doing to their bodies that it's no big deal. Is it?*

A. Yes, it is. Just consider some of the side effects.

First, alcohol lowers your inhibitions, which means you may say or do things you wish you hadn't. Also, alcohol is a "downer," which means it slows down your body's central nervous system. It can make you slur your speech, stagger when you walk, and bump into things. Because it's a downer, it also can cause depression. Some people drink to get out of a bad mood, but actually it only makes them feel worse.

A few other "BIG DEALS" about drinking:

☛ When the alcohol wears off, you may get what's known as a hangover, a reaction to having had too much to drink. You may feel dizzy or nauseated, have a headache, or feel tired and irritable.

☛ Alcohol is addicting. Once some people begin drinking, they can't stop, and they crave and drink alcohol every day.

☛ If you drink a lot of alcohol in a short period of time, you can pass out. You may not remember where you were or what you did. Sometimes you can even die.

☛ If you drink, then drive, or get in a car with someone who has been drinking, you put yourself at risk for being in an accident. Every year lots of kids die as victims of drunk-driving accidents.

Q. *My friend's father is an alcoholic. What exactly is alcoholism?*

A. This is a disease where people drink large amounts on a regular basis. They are unable to stop, even if they want to. Their craving for alcohol can take over their entire lives and cause them to lose everything they love, such as their jobs and their families.

Experts believe that alcoholism runs in families. If someone in your family is an alcoholic, you may be more at risk for the disease.

Alcoholism also can cause damage to the brain, pancreas, and kidneys; high blood pressure, heart attacks, and strokes; inflammation and scarring of the liver; stomach ulcers; and premature aging. Some people die from this disease.

There are many recovery programs available to help alcoholics kick their habit; however, even with help, stopping the drinking is very hard to do. Many recovered alcoholics struggle their entire lives with the desire to drink.

Q. *I've heard that it's impossible to be an alcoholic if you drink just beer or wine. Is this true?*

A. No. Beer and wine are just as addicting as any other alcohol. There are many alcoholics out there who primarily drink either of them.

By the way, you may have heard this because beer and wine are two drinks that a lot of kids consume, and maybe they are trying to rationalize their drinking. But don't believe it.

Q. *I went to a party the other night with some friends, and a few of the kids were drinking malt liquor. They told me it was just like drinking a soft drink. I had some and afterward felt weird. Does malt liquor have a lot of alcohol in it?*

A. It certainly does. In fact, **malt liquor is more potent than beer.** For example, four 12-ounce cans of malt liquor have as much alcohol as five to eight cans of beer. Plus, malt liquor is often served in single, 40-ounce containers. Kids buy these because they are cheap (they sell for as low as one dollar), then drink the entire bottle and wind up very drunk.

Q. *I'm confused. Some people say marijuana can't hurt you; others say it can. Which is true?*

A. What's true is that marijuana, also called pot or weed, can harm your body. Still, marijuana use is rising among teens. In fact, a 1997 study conducted by the National Institute on Drug Abuse (NIDA) showed that almost 50 percent of 12th graders had tried marijuana.

Smoking pot can do a lot of temporary damage to your body. When you use it you

◆ Have trouble thinking and remembering things.

◆ Lose coordination.

◆ Suffer from a dry mouth.

◆ Have bloodshot eyes.

◆ Experience an increased appetite, which can lead to unwanted weight gain.

In the long run, marijuana may cause permanent memory loss. It may also damage your lung tissue, give you symptoms of chronic bronchitis, and cause you to get more chest colds.

Q. *Is marijuana addictive? I've heard it isn't.*

A. You heard wrong. IT CAN BE VERY ADDICTIVE. More than 120,000 people seek treatment each year for marijuana use. Animal studies suggest marijuana causes physical dependence, and some people report withdrawal symptoms.

Q. *A kid at school told me you can take cocaine a few times without getting hooked. I thought cocaine was really addictive. Who is right?*

> **SOMETHING TO THINK ABOUT . . .**
>
> Research shows marijuana users tend to
>
> ✘ Be low achievers.
>
> ✘ Get into trouble more often.
>
> ✘ Show more anger and rebellion.
>
> ✘ Have poorer relationships with parents.
>
> ✘ Have more associations with delinquents and drug users.
>
> Many teens who wind up in drug treatment centers started using pot at an early age. All the more reason to never start!

A. You are. Cocaine, also called coke, is a powerfully addictive drug you can get hooked on after only using it once or twice.

Cocaine is a fine white powder usually inhaled through the nose. It also can be injected or smoked. Even though coke is very expensive, in recent years the number of teens who have tried it is increasing. (The NIDA reports 8.7 percent of high school seniors used cocaine at least once in 1997, compared with 5.9 in 1994.)

Cocaine makes people hyper, and they feel like they can do anything. But it also gives them the sweats, shakes, a racing heart rate, and a driving restlessness. After the drug wears off, users often feel depressed or anxious—so they reach for more.

Q. *What are some of the dangers of using cocaine?*

A. One of the biggest dangers is that once you are addicted, you will do almost anything to get more. People throw

away huge amounts of money on cocaine.
Or if they don't have the money, they may steal to get it.

Physically, cocaine can do major damage to your body. It can cause

✗ Dilated pupils and raised temperature, heart rate, and blood pressure.

✗ Chronic fatigue (the user is too wired to sleep).

✗ Chronic cough and nosebleeds.

✗ Paranoia (a state of mind where you think people are after you) and depression.

✗ Sinus and upper respiratory tract congestion and damage.

✗ Seizures, cardiac arrest, respiratory failure, and even death.

Q. *What is crack?*

A. Crack is a rock form of cocaine that is usually smoked. It is a much more concentrated form of the drug that rapidly reaches the brain and causes an immediate, intense high. Because of its immediate effects, crack is highly addictive.

Q. *I think a friend of mine might be doing drugs. Is there any way to tell?*

A. You may not be able to tell for sure, but there are a few telltale signs to look for. If you've noticed any of the following changes in her behavior, she may have a drug (or alcohol) problem:

❀ She disappears for periods of time, like at a party, with no explanation of where she's gone.

❄ She's dropped her usual activities and maybe even some of her friends. She's moody, seems tired a lot, and may be skipping school.

❄ She's lying a lot about what she's done and who she has been with. Her new friends tend to be kids who supposedly do drugs.

❄ She's fighting a lot with her parents.

❄ She's lost weight and looks sickly. If she's into pot or cocaine, she may cough a lot.

❄ She has trouble remembering things and acts "spacey" a lot of the time.

❄ She gets angry easily or acts paranoid.

If you suspect a pal is abusing drugs or alcohol, suggest that she get some help. If she won't, talk to your parents.

This is a problem that's
TOO BIG
for you to handle alone.

Your parents can talk to your friend's parents or other adults who are in a position to help her.

Q. *Does anyone still take heroin? Or was that just a drug of the 60s and 70s?*

A. Unfortunately, heroin is making a comeback. Since 1992, a growing number of people have become heroin addicts, reports the NIDA. A large portion of these new users were under the age of 26. Other reports show that young women are particularly at risk.

Heroin is a highly addictive narcotic that is either

smoked, snorted, or injected into the veins. Heroin causes many scary side effects, including

→ Delirium.

→ Shallow breathing.

→ Nausea.

→ Panic attacks.

→ Insomnia.

→ Collapsed veins.

→ Infection of the heart lining.

→ Liver disease.

→ Pneumonia.

→ The risk of contracting AIDS or hepatitis through shared needles.

→ Coma.

→ Overdose and death.

Q. *I've heard that sometimes kids get "high" on sniffing nail polish remover and glue. That sounds crazy.*

A. It is. But many kids use inhalants as cheap, accessible substitutes for alcohol. In fact, these are the most widely abused substances after alcohol, tobacco, and marijuana among eighth graders. And you won't believe the stuff they're sniffing:

✖ Paint thinner.

✖ Gasoline.

✖ Correction fluid.

IN 1997, MORE THAN
ONE IN FIVE
EIGHTH GRADERS USED
INHALANTS.

✖ Butane lighters.

✖ Whipped cream aerosols.

✖ Hair or deodorant sprays.

While sniffing these substances may seem harmless, it can kill you. Because the "high" these inhalants provide is short-lived (a few minutes or less), kids tend to inhale again and again. With each inhalation they feel less inhibited and yet in control. Finally, the user can lose consciousness.

Some inhalants can cause liver and kidney damage. Plus, inhalants can lead to these irreversible effects:

➜ Hearing loss.

➜ Limb spasms.

➜ Damage to the central nervous system or brain damage.

➜ Bone marrow damage.

Sniffing certain substances also can induce heart failure and DEATH.

Q. *What is ecstasy? I heard some kids talking about it at school.*

A. Ecstasy is a mind-altering drug that can cause severe anxiety. For several years, it has been a popular drug on the club and rock concert scenes. While at parties it is touted as a "fun" drug, there's nothing fun about ecstasy. Some side effects are:

⇀ Psychological problems, including confusion, depression, sleep problems, drug cravings, paranoia, and anxiety during and sometimes weeks after taking the drug.

⮑ Physical symptoms such as muscle tension, involuntary teeth clenching, nausea, blurred vision, rapid eye movement, faintness, chills, or sweating; also possibly an increase in heart rate and blood pressure.

Q. *A kid in school was using steroids to bulk up, but aren't steroids bad for you?*

A. They most certainly are. Unfortunately, some high school, college, and professional athletes get hooked on them as a way to increase their muscle mass and performance.

Steroids are synthetic derivatives of the male hormone testosterone. They are either taken orally or injected. In the short term, steroids increase lean muscle mass, strength, and the ability to train longer and harder. However, these gains come with risks. Steroid use can cause

➥ Liver tumors.

➥ Jaundice.

➥ High blood pressure.

➥ Trembling.

➥ Acne.

➥ Violent mood swings.

In adolescents, the drug can also halt growth prematurely.

Q. *Tell me about LSD. From what I've heard, it sounds really scary.*

A. LSD *is* scary. When people use it, they get supermoody and their judgment clouds over. They also experience hallucinations.

Hallucinations are vivid images that enter your mind while you are awake. Sometimes they are terrifying, just like nightmares. People on "bad trips" may panic so much they do crazy, dangerous things, like jump from buildings or run in front of cars. Plus once the drug has worn off, people can still get the hallucinations. These are called flashbacks, and they're another reason to never get mixed up with this drug.

OTHER DRUGS TO STAY AWAY FROM

"Speed": a powerful stimulant
Can cause nervousness, irritability, insomnia, nausea, hot flashes, sweating, heart palpitations, dryness of the mouth, confusion, severe anxiety, paranoia, death.

"Downers": depressants
Can cause disorientation, slurred speech, sedation, seizures, coma, heart failure, death.

"PCP": hallucinogenic drug
Can cause distortion of reality and possible memory loss, lack of concentration, decreased blood pressure, breathing problems, feelings of superhuman strength (which can cause a person to attempt a dangerous stunt), coma, death.

Q. *Can only illegal drugs hurt you?*

A. No. Almost any drug can hurt you if you take too much or take the wrong prescription. For example, **even LARGE amounts of ASPIRIN can KILL you.**

For this reason, never take more than the prescribed dosage of a medicine, and never, ever experiment with someone else's medication (such as some pills you find in a medicine cabinet).

Q. *How do I say no when someone is pressuring me to do drugs or drink?*

A. There are two main pointers to remember when resisting peer pressure: Be consistent and be firm.

Let it be known up front that you are not the sort of person who drinks or does drugs. Stick to your principles in all situations. If you are consistent, people will not pressure you as much because they know their pleadings will fall on deaf ears.

Also, when you do say no, say it like you mean it. You don't have to make a big deal of it or give a speech on sobriety. In a calm, firm voice, simply say, *"No, thank you. I don't drink (or do drugs)."* If you are firm and act confidently about your choice, people will not question it.

Two other tips: Don't put yourself in situations where drugs and alcohol will be available. For example, if a friend is having an unsupervised party, pass on attending it. Also, find friends who share your values and don't drink or do drugs either. That way you won't be forced to constantly defend your values and principles.

Q. *Smoking seems so gross, but a lot of kids I know do it. Last week at a family reunion—I couldn't believe it—two of my cousins snuck away and were smoking. Do a lot more teens these days smoke than in the past?*

A. Yep, the number *is* on the rise. According to a recent study by the Office on Smoking and Health, a division of the Centers for Disease Control, nearly half (48.2 percent) of male high school students and more than a third (36 percent) of female students reported using some form of tobacco—cigarette, cigar, or smokeless tobacco—in the past month.

The bad news is that SMOKING is highly ADDICTIVE.

If you start young, chances are, you'll keep smoking. Among adult smokers, 80 percent smoked their first cigarette before their 18th birthday—and by that time, 50 percent were smoking daily. That's because breaking the smoking habit is extremely hard for people to do.

In fact, about three-fourths of young people who smoke daily say they continue to do so because "it is really hard for them to quit."

SEVENTY PERCENT OF ADOLESCENT SMOKERS WISH THEY HAD NEVER STARTED SMOKING IN THE FIRST PLACE.

And get this: Each day in the United States, more than 3,000 young people become regular smokers—more than one million new smokers a year. Of these, nearly one-third will die prematurely of a smoking-related disease.

Q. *Why is smoking so dangerous?*

A. When you take a puff on a cigarette, you are putting potentially deadly gases, such as carbon monoxide and tar, directly into your lungs. The tar exposes the user to lung cancer, emphysema, and bronchial problems. The carbon monoxide puts smokers at risk for cardiovascular disease. In addition, smoking causes special problems for young people, reports the Office on Smoking and Health:

✓ Smoking limits your fitness level. You aren't able to run as fast or as far.

✓ Smoking can hamper the rate of lung growth and the level of maximum lung function.

✓ The resting heart rate of young adult smokers is two to three beats per minute faster than that of nonsmokers.

✓ You put yourself at risk for constant cough and increased respiratory illnesses.

As if this weren't enough, high school seniors who are regular smokers and who begin by ninth grade are

✗ 2.4 times more likely than nonsmokers to report poorer overall health.

✗ 2.4 to 2.7 percent more likely to report cough with phlegm or blood, shortness of breath when not exercising, and wheezing or gasping.

✘ 3.0 times more likely to have seen a doctor or other health professional for an emotional or psychological complaint.

Whew! There are so many good reasons not to smoke that it's amazing anyone does.

Q. *I've heard about secondhand smoke. Is it as dangerous as everyone says it is?*

A. Yes. When people smoke, they aren't only putting themselves at risk but also those around them. The Environmental Protection Agency has concluded that secondhand smoke causes lung cancer in adults and greatly increases the risk of respiratory illnesses in children as well as sudden infant death. More good reasons to never take that first puff!

Learn MORE!

Talk to some adults who smoke and/or who have recovered from an alcohol or drug addiction. Ask them how and why they started and also about the negative side effects they have experienced (or are experiencing). What advice would they give you?

Sometimes it's hard to know how truly bad something is for you until you talk to people who have been "in the trenches" and suffered an alcohol, drug, or tobacco addiction. Their stories can further your resolve to steer clear of any of these dangerous substances.

$\mathcal{B}$eauty Problems Solved

From the time I could remember, I bit my nails. They were stubby, horrible things, bitten down as far as humanly possible. When I reached the seventh grade, I began to notice not everyone's nails looked like mine. Many girls had nice, long, shapely nails. Others wore polish. I felt like hiding mine in gloves year-round.

I decided to stop biting my nails. But it was tougher than I thought, and I kept nibbling. One day I found some old medicine in the cabinet that my mom had used years ago when I was a toddler to cure me of sucking my thumb. It was supposed to taste so terrible, you'd never want to put your fingers in your mouth again.

I doused the stuff all over my nails. Five minutes later, I took my first bite—and almost puked. Maybe the stuff really was horrible tasting, or maybe it had fermented during all the years it had sat there, but I thought I was going to die. I practically had to wash my mouth out with soap to get the taste out.

There went that solution to my beauty problem. I resolved that people would have to like me, raggedy nails and all. It took me another 20 years before I finally kicked the nail-biting habit!

Q. *My skin is really oily. I hate it because it makes my face so shiny. I look like I'm sweating all the time. What should I do?*

A. Having oily skin doesn't have to wreck your beauty—or your mood! Your skin contains something called sebaceous glands, which produce sebum, a waxy lubricant. If you have oily skin, it means that your glands produce more sebum than other people's do. The good news is, your skin is well moisturized and, as you get older, less likely to develop wrinkles.

To combat an oily complexion, try these tips:

❧ **Wash your face at least two times a day** (more can be irritating to your skin) with a drying soap designed for oily skin.

❧ **Use an oil-free moisturizer,** which feels less greasy than one containing oil.

❧ **Carry some tissues around with you during the day to pat your face dry.** If your face gets shiny, duck into the bathroom to do this.

❧ **Use a toner.** This product removes excess surface cells, soap residues, and oils from your skin.

❧ If your parents say it's OK to wear makeup, **use face powder,** either loose or in a compact, to cover the shine. Put some on in the morning before you leave the house; then dab on a light layer whenever your skin gets that certain glow.

Q. *My skin is superdry. It gets chapped easily and looks really ugly. Do you have any suggestions on how to have smoother skin?*

A. A few changes in your beauty routine will help "smooth" the way for less-dry skin:

> ❥ **Don't wash your face more than you have to,** and when you do, use warm instead of hot water. Both cleansing and hot water can rob skin of its natural oils.

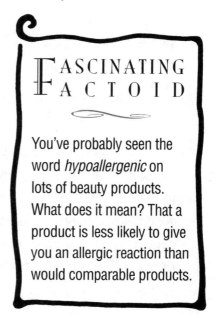

FASCINATING **F**ACTOID

You've probably seen the word *hypoallergenic* on lots of beauty products. What does it mean? That a product is less likely to give you an allergic reaction than would comparable products.

> ❥ **Use a superfatted soap.** This contains extra fatty substances to help your skin not dry out as much when you wash it.

> ❥ **Wear a moisturizer every day.** Moisturizers work by trapping water on the skin, which helps keep it smooth and moist. If your skin is superdry and acne isn't a problem, petroleum jelly can make a great moisturizer. But only use it at night—it's too greasy to use during the day.

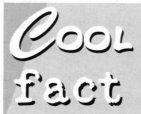

Cool fact

The very first moisturizer was olive oil, used some 6,000 years ago.

Q. *I've been popping my pimples, but my mom tells me that's bad for my skin. Why?*

A. When you pop, pick, or poke at a pimple, it increases the inflammation and can make your skin even more red and swollen. Plus, if the skin becomes inflamed enough, you could be left with acne scars. *So listen to your mother!*

Q. *Sunblock seems so oily. Should I keep using it even though I'm getting pimples?*

A. Yes. Doctors recommend that people of all ages wear a sunblock with an SPF of 15 every day, rain or shine (sun filters in through the clouds). *Sunblock is your insurance against sun damage and cancer.* Yes, some products are oily, but there are several on the market designed specifically to be used on the face that are not greasy. They are added to moisturizers for use on your face every morning year-round.

Q. *How important is it when I break out to keep my face clean?*

A. While keeping your face clean won't prevent acne, it can help you control it. Here are some tips to follow:

✳ **Wash pimple-prone areas with warm water and a mild soap two times a day.** If you can't get to a sink to suds up, use a nonoily cleansing lotion that you just smear on, then wipe off.

✳ If you have extra-oily skin, **remove any excess oil after washing by dipping a cotton ball in an astringent** and gently wiping the cotton ball over trouble spots.

✳ **Select noncomedogenic (non acne-forming) makeup.** Makeup manufacturers will have this information on their product packaging. Try not to use base makeup.

✳ **Remove all makeup from your face each night** or immediately after school if possible.

✳ **Keep your hair off your face.**

Q. *I've heard that eating chocolate as well as fried, fatty foods and junk food can cause pimples. Is this true?*

A. There is no scientific evidence to support the notion that specific foods have an effect on the skin. However, don't use this information as an excuse to go out and eat a lot of these basically unhealthy foods!

Q. *In the summer, my complexion seems to clear up. Is this because I'm in the sun more often?*

A. Maybe. Many people's skin is helped by a dry, warm climate, but that's not true for every-

Your skin is the largest organ of your body, covering, on average, two yards.

one. Some people's acne actually gets worse in the summer, especially if they sweat a lot.

Q. *I started getting my first pimples last year, but only a few of them. Now they are popping up fast and furiously. It's disgusting. Should I see a doctor about this?*

A. If more than a few pimples crop up, it's best to see your doctor. If necessary, he or she can give you treatments to help your skin or refer you to a skin doctor, called a dermatologist, for further treatment.

Q. *What kinds of products and treatments are available to help combat acne?*

A. There are many different treatments available, which are discussed below. However, before you use any of these products, consult a dermatologist. He or she can help determine which one will be the safest and most effective for you. The doctor can also oversee your treatment to make sure you are using the products to get the best results.

➡ **Hydroxy acids.** These over-the-counter products remove excess cells from your skin's surface, which helps open blocked pores. This is a good place to start if you have mild acne, and you should try it for a few months to determine how well it works.

➡ **Benzoyl peroxide.** Products containing this are available both over-the-counter and by prescription in lotion, gel, and cream forms. Such products dry out your skin and fight the bacteria that causes blemishes. They are most effective on mild acne.

Benzoyl peroxide products come in several different concentrations. It's best to start with a low concentration. If that doesn't work, you can move up to the next highest level. But you will want to wait at least three to four weeks before moving up. Also, never use a higher concentration without first checking with your doctor.

These products can dry out and/or irritate your skin. If your skin becomes very red or itchy, stop using them and consult your dermatologist.

➡ **Retin-A®.** Retin-A® is a prescription medication for mild-to-moderate acne, which unplugs follicles and stops them from clogging in the first place.

Retin-A® comes in many strengths. Your dermatologist will probably start you off with a low-concentration level.

Retin-A® can cause your skin to become red and irritated. Also, it will take several months of use to see if it is effective on your skin.

➥ **Topical antibiotics.** These prescription medications are designed for mild-to-moderate acne. They work by stopping the growth of the bacteria that contribute to acne. The most common antibiotics used are clindamycin, erythromycin, and tetracycline.

Your doctor will probably suggest you apply them once or twice a day.

➥ **Oral antibiotics.** Your dermatologist may prescribe tetracycline or another antibiotic in a pill or liquid form if the topical medication isn't working. These products can be effective but can cause side effects, such as an upset stomach and headaches.

Q. *Summer is almost here, and I will be wearing a bikini soon. Problem is, when I went to try on my suit, I realized some of my pubic hair was showing. Help!*

A. You may want to shave around your pubic hair area (with the permission of your parents, of course) so that none of the hair shows when you are in your bathing suit.

There are several ways to remove unwanted hair. Most girls opt for shaving. An electric razor is easier to use, but a blade razor will give you the smoothest shave.

Other ways to remove hair involve chemicals, wax, or

electric currents. These can be irritating to the skin and so need to be done with extra care by a professional. For this reason, it's best to stick with shaving.

Q. *The other day I tried to use a blade razor on my legs, and I ended up with dozens of nicks and cuts. It was a mess! How can I make sure this doesn't happen again?*

A. By being very careful! Here are some safety tips to follow:

✳ Soak your skin well in warm water before shaving (or shave during or after a bath or shower). That way, your skin will be softer and the hairs easier to cut.

✳ Consider spreading shaving cream on the areas you want to shave, which makes the razor glide more smoothly over your skin. Soap can also do the trick.

✳ Shave up the leg, not down.

✳ Use long, slow strokes. *Don't feel you're trying to* **beat the clock** *when you shave* or you will end up with nicks and cuts. Pay special attention to the sensitive areas of the shin bone, ankle, and knee.

✳ When shaving your pubic area, be especially careful, as this area is delicate and can easily become irritated.

✳ Use a moisturizer on your legs between shaves to cut down on skin dryness or irritation.

Q. *My best friend and I just bought a bunch of products to help us with our new perspiration problem. What's the difference between a deodorant and an antiperspirant, and what is the best way to use them?*

A. No sweat; here's the scoop:

Deodorants cover up with a fragrance any odor from perspiration. Antiperspirants are more effective because they plug the openings of your armpit sweat glands, thus blocking perspiration from reaching the skin's surface. You can also find dual antiperspirants/deodorants on the market. Some doctors recommend deodorants, which don't stop your body from sweating and are natural and healthy.

(Deodorants just cover up the ODOR!)

Always apply a deodorant or antiperspirant after a shower so your body won't have time to work up a sweat. However, make sure the area under your arm is completely dry before applying the product or it may wash away.

Also, make sure to wait a few minutes before dressing or the deodorant or antiperspirant may rub off on your clothes. If you start to work up a sweat later in the day, reapply the product as needed.

Q. *I never use a conditioner on my hair. My best friend says that I'm crazy and that my hair will never look as good as it could. Is she right? Are conditioners that important?*

A. If your hair is naturally very oily, you may not need one, but most people's hair does benefit from a conditioner. Conditioner can help your locks from drying out and looking limp and flat. Just make sure you read the directions on the back of the bottle carefully. Some conditioners are supposed to be rinsed out, others kept in your hair.

Q. *The other day I looked in the mirror and saw I had dandruff. I almost died. I kept brushing it off, but it kept reappearing. What can I do to solve this terrible problem?*

A. You may be using too much hairspray or other styling products that are flaking off and doing a good dandruff imitation. Or perhaps your scalp is dry. If your hair products don't seem to be the culprit, switch to a dandruff shampoo that is designed to control scalp flaking.

Q. *I hear that too much blow-drying can wreck your hair because it dries it out. Well, I'm in trouble because I blow-dry mine every day. Can you give me some pointers on how I can have healthy blow-dried hair?*

A. **"HAIR'S" THE LOWDOWN:** Blow-dry your hair when it's damp, not soaking wet, to minimize the amount of time you are drying it. Choose a medium instead of high-heat setting, and stop blow-drying before your hair is completely dry.

Q. *I finally quit biting my nails. But the bummer is, they won't grow. As soon as they get to a certain length, they chip off. What can I do?*

A. Sounds like you are a good candidate for a nail strengthener. This works by penetrating and hardening the nails. You may also want to use a cuticle conditioner, since healthy growth starts at the cuticle.

Also, as soon as a nail chips, smooth it down with a buffer to preserve what length is left until the nail grows out.

Q. *My mom finally said I can wear a little blush. But when I* *put it on, I look like a big strawberry. How should I be applying it?*

A. For starters, select a color that complements your complexion. Your mom or the salesperson behind the cosmetic counter can help you pick out the right shade.

Second, select a powder blush. Blush also comes in gel or cream forms, but these are hard to blend evenly and can look blotchy.

Apply the blusher along your cheekbone, starting at the middle of your cheek and brushing upward. Sometimes it helps to use a big brush instead of the small one provided with the product, because a bigger brush helps the blush go on smoothly.

Q. *My mom says I can't wear makeup until I'm 16. Help! I'm 13 and I want to wear it now. All my friends do, and I feel like a dweeb not being able to.*

A. While it's tough not being able to do what other kids do, remember, it's what's inside, not your appearance, that's important, and determines whether or not you are a dweeb (AND I'M SURE YOU'RE NOT!).

On the other hand, many preteens and teens do wear some makeup. Ask your mom if you can at least wear lip gloss or very light lipstick. If you start small (as opposed to running out and buying a bright red lipstick), your mom may be more accepting of your wearing makeup.

Q. *I want to dye my hair this cool maroon color. My parents say no way. What do you think?*

A. Dying can take a big toll on your hair. It can dry it out, making it brittle and frizzy. Sometimes once you start dying, you can't stop and are always looking for the "perfect color." Often girls and women dye their hair for years, then go back to their original color. And when they do, they often like it so much, they wonder why they ever switched in the first place.

Why don't you compromise with your parents and put in a temporary color that washes out? **You can see if you like the color,** and your parents will like the fact that the color won't last forever.

Q. *All of my friends have pierced ears. Some of them even have their noses pierced. What do you think? Should I pierce or shouldn't I?*

A. There's nothing wrong with piercing your ears as long as you take good care of them. However, wait a while before you decide to pierce your nose—or any other body part, for that matter.

Face and body piercing can be painful, and while you may think the look is cool, soon you may grow tired of it and wish you hadn't done it.

Q. *Even though I am still eating the same amount as always, I've started to gain weight. Some of the changes I like, but others I don't.*

A. During puberty, not only are you growing taller, you're filling out too. Suddenly, you've got curves. Your hips become rounded, and so does your rear. Your face will probably start filling out as well.

While these changes are new and therefore disconcerting, keep in mind that it's normal for girls to have a 10 to 20 percent weight increase during puberty, mostly due to an increase in body fat. This weight gain is to be expected and means you are healthy. It does not mean you need to lose weight. With time, as you grow used to your new look, you will feel more comfortable with it.

Q. *The other day I looked in the mirror and, for the first time, saw some cellulite on my thighs. How gross! What can I do to get rid of it—fast?*

A. While you may have read about products that claim to banish **cellulite** forever, actually, there's nothing you can do about it—except try not to let it worry you so much. Lots of girls and women have some on their bodies.

Despite its fancy name, **cellulite is just ordinary fat** that develops below the buttocks. The best way to lose fat is to eat a well-rounded, low-fat diet and get regular exercise.

Q. *If you had just one beauty tip to give girls, what would it be?*

A. *To smile.* I know that sounds corny, but a smiling face is twice as pretty as a frowning one. As an added bonus, studies show that people who smile a lot are perceived as nicer and kinder *and* are more popular.

Learn MORE!

• •

While it's true that puberty brings along some overwhelming changes, some of which you are uncomfortable with, it also is the start of many wonderful things. You already know what you don't like about puberty; so now write down the things that you do enjoy. Maybe it's getting breasts, feeling more grown-up, or watching your figure turn more feminine. The more you concentrate on the "improvements," the less you'll focus on the "drawbacks" of puberty.

LOSSARY

adrenal glands (uh-DREE-nuhl GLANDS): Glands that produce androgens, the hormones that turn on sweat glands and cause other changes during puberty.

aerobic (air-OH-bik): Any activity that allows a person to raise his or her heart rate. Aerobic exercise is an efficient way to burn fat and keep your heart and lungs in shape.

alveoli (al-VEE-uh-lee): The tiny structures in the breast that produce milk for babies.

amenorrhea (uh-meh-nuh-REE-uh): Absence of the regular monthly menstrual cycle.

androgens (AN-druh-juhnz): Male sex hormones that both men and women produce. During puberty, they are the hormones that turn on the sweat glands and produce other changes.

anorexia nervosa (an-uh-REK-see-uh ner-VOH-suh): An eating disorder that causes people to starve themselves in an attempt to stay thin.

areola (uh-REE-uh-luh): The round, pinkish-brown area around the nipple on a breast.

breasts (BRESTS): Two glands located on the chest wall containing the glands that produce milk for babies. Girls begin developing breasts during puberty.

bulimia nervosa (boo-LEE-mee-uh ner-VOH-suh): An eating disorder that causes people to binge on food, then purge it through vomiting, laxatives, diuretics, or exercise.

cellulite (SELL-yuh-lite): Lumpy body fat found in the thighs, hips, and buttocks of some girls and women.

cervix (SER-viks): The narrow outer end of the uterus that joins with the vagina.

cholesterol (kuh-LES-tuh-roll): A waxy, fatty substance found in animal cells and body fluids.

cilia (SIH-lee-uh): The tiny hairs that line the fallopian tubes.

clitoris (KLIH-tuh-rus): A small, knoblike organ in the female's vulva.

corpus luteum (KOR-pus LOO-tee-um): A yellowish tissue from which the hormone progesterone is released after ovulation.

dysmenorrhea (diss-meh-nuh-REE-uh): Painful periods.

ejaculation (ih-jak-yoo-LAY-shun): The discharge of semen from the penis once the man reaches climax.

endometrium (en-doh-MEE-tree-um): The innermost lining of the uterus.

epididymis (eh-puh-DIH-duh-mus): The mass of tubes that carries sperm from the testes to the vas deferens in the male body.

erection (ih-REK-shun): The swelling and hardening of the penis when a male becomes sexually excited. The swelling and hardening is caused by the flow of blood into the tissues of the penis.

estrogen (ESS-truh-jun): One of the several hormones that causes many of the physical changes girls experience during puberty. It is produced in the ovaries.

fallopian tubes (fuh-LOH-pee-un TOOBS): One of the two ducts that leads from the top of the uterus to one of the two ovaries. The fallopian tube is open by the ovary, and this is usually where an egg is fertilized by a sperm.

fertilization (fir-tuhl-uh-ZAY-shun): The process in which a sperm joins with an egg. Pregnancy begins at fertilization.

fimbriae (FIM-bree-ee): The hairlike fringes that border the entrance to the fallopian tubes.

follicle-stimulating hormone (FSH) (FAH-lih-kuhl): One of the hormones associated with the initiation of puberty.

Gonadotropin-releasing hormone (GnRh) (go-nad-uh-TROH-puhn): One of the hormones associated with the initiation of puberty.

hormones (HOR-mohnz): A wide variety of protein molecules that are produced and released from special glands in the body.

hymen (HY-mun): The membrane that partially covers the vaginal opening.

hypothalamus (hy-poh-THAL-uh-mus): A structure in the brain that produces the substance Gonadotropin-releasing hormone (GnRh), which is involved in the onset of puberty.

iron-deficiency anemia (I-ern dih-FIH-shun-see uh-NEE-mee-uh): A disease of decreased red blood cell mass caused by lack of iron in the body.

labia majora (LAY-bee-uh muh-JOR-uh): The outer lips of the vulva, outside the vagina.

labia minora (LAY-bee-uh muh-NOR-uh): The inner lips of the vulva, on either side of the vaginal opening.

lobes (LOHBZ): Several separate milk-producing units that are found in each breast.

luteinizing hormone (LH) (LEW-tee-uh-neye-zing HOR-mohn): One of the hormones associated with the initiation of puberty.

menarche (MEH-nar-kee): The onset of menstruation.

menopause (MEH-nuh-pawz): The time of life when a woman stops menstruating.

menstruation (men-stroo-WAY-shun): The monthly passage of blood and tissue through the vagina.

menstrual cycle (MEN-strool SY-kul): The monthly reproductive cycle for a female.

milk ducts (MIHLK DUKTS): The milk-carrying tubes that lead from the alveoli, or milk glands, to small openings on the surface of the nipples.

mons pubis (MONZ PYOO-buhs): The fatty tissue that covers the pubic bone.

myometrium (my-uh-MEE-tree-um): The muscular middle layer of the uterine wall that contracts during menstruation. During birth, the contractions of this muscle help push the baby out.

obesity (oh-BEE-suh-tee): A condition where a person is excessively overweight.

ovaries (OH-vuh-reez): The two almond-shaped organs in the female reproductive system. The ovaries contain all the egg cells needed for a lifetime of reproduction.

ovulation (ahv-yoo-LAY-shun): The process in which an egg is released from one of the ovaries and begins to travel to the uterus. Ovulation usually occurs once a month.

ovum (OH-vum): A female's reproductive cell, or egg.

pectoral (PEK-tuh-ruhl): Referring to the chest area.

penis (PEE-nus): A male's external sexual organ.

pituitary gland (puh-TOO-uh-ter-ee GLAND): The structure within the brain that produces several hormones including FSH and LH.

progesterone (proh-JES-tuh-rohn): A hormone produced by the corpus luteum, progesterone causes some of the physical changes girls experience during puberty. It is also important in regulating a girl's monthly menstrual cycle and in maintaining pregnancy.

prostaglandins (prahs-tuh-GLAN-dunz): Hormonelike chemicals that cause the muscle in the uterus to contract during menstruation.

puberty (PYOO-ber-tee): The physical and emotional changes that take place in everyone between childhood and adulthood.

scrotum (SKROH-tum): The sack of skin that holds the testicles and hangs down behind a male's penis.

semen (SEE-mun): A liquid made up of sperm and fluid that is released from the penis when a man ejaculates.

serosa (suh-ROH-zuh): The smooth outer covering of the uterus.

serotonin (sihr-uh-TOE-nihn): A brain chemical associated with regulating mood and energy levels.

sperm (SPURM): A male's reproductive cell, also called spermatozoon (spur-ma-tuh-ZOH-ahn).

staphylococcus aureus (staf-uh-loh-KAH-kus OR-ee-us): The bacterium that is believed to cause toxic shock syndrome.

STD: The acronym for sexually transmitted diseases. An STD is passed from person to person by intimate or sexual contact. Some STDs include genital warts, herpes, and AIDS.

target heart rate: This is the rate at which your heart rate should beat during exercise to receive the maximum benefit. To find your target heart rate, subtract your age from 220. Then multiply that number by .75.

testicles (TESS-tih-kulz): The two small egg-shaped organs inside the male scrotum that produce sperm.

testosterone (tess-TOSS-tuh-rohn): The main male hormone.

toxic shock syndrome: Also known as TSS, this is a disease that has been linked to tampon use.

urethra (yoo-REE-thruh): The tube leading from the bladder to the outside of the body through which urine passes.

uterus (YOO-tuh-rus): An upside-down pear-shaped organ, located in the woman's pelvis, that is for holding and nourishing a baby prior to birth.

vagina (vuh-JY-nuh): The canal that leads from the uterus to the outside of the female's body. During menstruation, blood and tissue pass through this canal.

vaginitis (va-juh-NY-tus): An inflammation of the vagina.

vas deferens (VASS DEF-uh-runz): A tube in the male body that carries sperm from the epididymis to the ejaculatory duct.

vulva (VUHL-vuh): The genital organs on the outside of the female body.

zygote (ZY-goht): A fertilized egg.

INDEX

*A*BOUT THE AUTHOR

Alison Bell, the author of *Your Body, Yourself,* is a former columnist and associate managing editor at *'TEEN* magazine. Her other midgrade titles for girls like you include *Ask Allie, The Dream Scene,* and *How to Analyze Handwriting.* She has written for such other national magazines as *YM, Women's Sports and Fitness,* and *New Body.* She lives with her husband and two children in South Pasadena, California.

Look for her latest book, *Your Beauty, Your Health, Yourself,* to be published in the spring of 2000.